A PASSAGE
THROUGH
DIVORCE

A PASSAGE THROUGH DIVORCE

BARBARA BAUMGARDNER

BROADMAN
&HOLMAN
PUBLISHERS

Nashville, Tennessee

0-8054-1117-8

Published by Broadman & Holman Publishers
Nashville, Tennessee
Editorial Team: Vicki Crumpton,
Janis Whipple, Kim Overcash
Page Design: Desktop Miracles, Inc., Dallas, Texas
Cover Design: Left Coast Design, Inc., Portland, Oregon

1 2 3 4 5 03 02 01 00 99

Dedication

To Jan Mathers and Betty Grimshaw:
priceless friends and gifted writers who
consistently critique my work with loving honesty.
For your valuable input and encouragement,
I say thank you, thank you.
You are the wind beneath my writer's wings.

To each person who trusted me with your broken heart
and shattered life for the stories recorded herein,
I offer my sincere gratitude.
I pray that your journey will be paved with
exhilarating joy and God's undeniable love.
Take His hand and my hug.

Contents

Introduction		*ix*
Session 1:	Journaling My Way through Divorce	1
Session 2:	Responses to Divorce Grief	25
Session 3:	Facing Firsts	43
Session 4:	Dear Ex	63
Session 5:	Creatively Speaking	81
Session 6:	Holidays and Special Days	97
Session 7:	Moving On!	115
Epilogue		127
Leader's Guide (for group use)		133
Suggested Reading		161
Endnotes		162

Introduction

Dear Friend:

It is important to me that you know I've walked in your shoes. I've known the agony of rejection that clings like spider webs after a divorce. I remember the damp chill of loneliness that creeps in when you least expect it. Like me, you may be asking, "Does anyone care?"

I care.

And God cares.

On my own journey through the valley of the shadow of divorce, hope emerged when I found that God, whom I feared had forgotten me, was there all the time. I discovered He truly was in the dark places of my pain. He came to me as I wrote words in my journal—pain-coated words about my anger, my fears, and my confusion.

I pray that you'll find Him, too, in the deep, dark crevices of your divorce and that your journey through this workbook will end in hope and healing.

Reach up and take hold of His hand before turning to the next page.

Barbara Baumgardner

Your Name _____

Telephone_____

Date _____

Journaling My Way through Divorce

— ❧ —

There are two ways of meeting difficulties:
you alter the difficulties or you alter
yourself meeting them.

Phyllis Bottome

— ❧ —

My Marriage Has Ended

My marriage has ended,
and everything has changed
by this event.
I am painfully aware
that life
can never be the same again;
that yesterday is over,
that loving relationship I thought
would last a lifetime
is finished.
But there is another way
to look upon this truth.
If my heart did not hurt
and my eyes did not weep,
I could only conclude
that I was incapable of loving
and that my marriage,
though failed,
meant nothing.
The fact that I am hurting
tells me I am still alive,
for it is only the dead who stop hurting.
Life can never be the same,
but life can be different and good
because God is good,
and for that fact alone, I will risk
stepping out to face my future
without dwelling on my past.[1]

Understanding the Process of Journaling

If some aspects of your divorce are too difficult to talk about, or if you seem to be stuck at some point in getting on with your life, you may find that the act of writing out your thoughts will help you clarify and come to grips with them.

This process is called "journaling." Hopefully, this book will become your road map and guide into the concept of journaling your way to wholeness. Journaling can be an important step toward maintaining good mental health while feelings of rejection, disappointment, and guilt disrupt your peace. It is especially helpful in the dark of the night, when loneliness seems to intensify and sleep eludes you. Writing is particularly useful for those people who didn't want to say good-bye to their marriage.

You can write anytime you need to talk. It is a safe way to discharge anger that might otherwise be directed toward someone who has disappointed you.

Journaling can diminish guilt feelings and be a more comfortable way to unload sorrow and memories that you are not willing to share with another human being.

Another reason to write is to preserve the good memories instead of dwelling only on the bad ones. Sometimes the good memories get lost in the struggles of a divorce, but they are there—just as the reason you married this person in the first place is there—valid and valuable.

There is no time limit or expectation for completing your journaling book. No one will judge you or your writing abilities as you complete it in your own unique way. If you are participating in a divorce support group, you will be pleased to soon find yourself comfortable with the concept of sharing and reading aloud. Hopefully, you will find refuge in meeting with other people under the shelter of God's love.

If you are taking your journey through this book alone, don't hurry. Pause to pray often, and take time as needed to reflect and heal amidst the recording of your progress. I hope you'll find journaling is a pleasant experience that never ends as paper and pencil become your companion and friend.

Determine to allow your pain to flow freely onto a piece of paper. Once you write it down, you can more easily set it free. Anticipate the day when you will no longer hold on to your bitterness or feelings of failure but release them forever. It will be then that joy and peace can take up residency in your once fragmented life.

Beginning

Take a few moments to be still before God. Listen as He reminds you that He is able and willing to help you carry your burdens. Matthew 11:28–30 says, "Come to me, all you who are weary and burdened, and I will give you rest. Take my yoke upon you and learn from me, for I am gentle and humble in heart, and you will find rest for your souls. For my yoke is easy and my burden is light."

What a great prescription for *soul pain!* Someone once told me that a yoke is usually custom made. Because it is made for me, it fits perfectly! And it is His strength, not mine, that will carry the burden. I know I can count on that, and so can you!

Don't be embarrassed if emotions and tears find their way to the surface. They are part of the healing process.

Think about your loss of a mate and the hole it left in your life. Even if you are the one who instigated the divorce with very valid reasons, it still leaves a hole. Name that hole. Say his or her name aloud.

This is not the time to review the reactions of other people or to dwell upon details that led to the severance of your marriage vows. This is a time to examine yourself in light of the loss of relationship with your husband or wife. It is a time to draw close to the Lord so He can draw close to you.

If you are unable to talk or write about your divorce in this journal, ask yourself if you are stuffing your feelings down inside instead of freeing them to heal.

How long did you know your spouse before marriage? _4-5 yrs_

How many years were you married? _18 yrs_

Was this divorce sudden or expected? _Sudden_

How are you coping with the loss, and what help are you getting?

At times I'm fine. Other times, like now I am very depressed, confused, scared.

What are your expectations from this journaling book?

To help me deal with the divorce so I can move on with my life

If you are in a group setting, use the following lines to write down the names of others in your group as you each introduce yourselves and answer the above questions. Note something you want to remember about each of them.

If you are soloing through this journal, use the following lines for additional space in answering the above questions if needed. Describe who you are now that this divorce is final and how it has changed you.

_____

_____

_____

You may be experiencing grief as though a death has occurred. There is grief in divorce. Your grief will be like no one else's. It will be unique and, though shared with others, should not be compared with others.

— ❦ —

You grieve differently from other people—not
so differently that you cannot find fellowship
in suffering with them, yet so differently that
no one else's grief is exactly like your own.
Wayne E. Oates[2]

— ❦ —

Sometimes we don't understand exactly how we feel until we see what we think on paper. To begin your journaling, pick up your pencil. Think about one experience (happy or unpleasant) you had with your former mate. Don't worry about form or punctuation or spelling. Begin by making some brief notes in the form of an outline, and then go back and fill in the details. Feel free to rewrite, cross out, erase, or fill in. This outline will help you to begin.

An incident you remember:

When Don got so mad at Blake because he wasn't reading right. Don started spanking him very hard I had to step in.

Describe the day:

Don had worked on the house at night after working all day

The setting:

We were in Blake's room at my parents house

The sounds:

TV in the background

The smells:

?

The prevailing emotions:

Anger, Embarassment, disgust, broken heart for Blake

The people involved:

Me, Don, Blake
My parents were in another room.

Now, using the outline, tell the whole story. Add pages if needed. This writing is best done when you are all alone, enabling your emotions to flow freely without the distraction of sympathy or audience.

Date: I wanted Don to help with the Kids. I wanted him to hear Blake reading. Blake was 6 in ~~first~~ Kindegarten. Blake didn't want to read. He quit trying he was afraid he'd get something wrong. Don got mad. He told Blake he had to read. When Blake wouldn't, Don started to spank him really hard.

Don wouldn't stop. He kept on spanking with all his might until I physically got in between them. I was so angry at Don + so hurt for Blake. I was embarassed because I thought my parents could hear what was going on. I told Don to never, ever do that again. I just sat and held Blake while he cried. Don went to bed. I hated him for that

In every winter's heart,
there is a quivering spring,
and behind the veil of each night
there is a smiling dawn.

Kahil Gibran[3]

Putting Divorce into Words

How would you describe divorce? After his divorce, columnist Chris Cox reflected on the experience. He wrote:

> Is it a monument to personal failure, a symbol of your lack of resolve and character, a gaudy trophy of your poor choices, a scrap heap of busted dreams? Or is it another chance, a fresh start, an opportunity for growth and an occasion for courage?
>
> Divorce is a bomb that blows to shreds your sense of who you are and what you have become. It is a series of land mines, going off in your face when you least expect, the shrapnel of memories searing your heart. Little remnants of you, barely recognizable in the wake of each blast, float scattered about the breeze as dandelion fluff; they are no longer organized around anything and they take no form, assume no familiar shape. The center around which your life has been defined is suddenly gone and utterly ripped away. It is as if someone has given you a jigsaw puzzle of your life, removed half the pieces, and still expects you to form a coherent whole.
>
> Divorce creates a radical new context for the past. Suddenly old Polaroids of vacations and anniversaries aren't reference points—they take on the weight of historical significance. With no warning whatsoever, ordinary household objects become animate creatures, fluent in the language of loss, alive with symbolic value.

This shirt represents that crazy day at the mall when we got harassed by the sales clerk who looked exactly like an Afghan hound. Here are the candles, half-burned and coated in light dust, which you loved to light on rainy nights. This is the drawer in which we hoarded coupons we would never use. This casserole dish, which has seen how many nights of meals, how many noble experiments (chicken pot pie with oregano), how many washings and dryings. This window, which we looked out one cold February afternoon and saw a cardinal, its brilliant red color a frail complaint against the gray, overcast sky and we discussed the end of our marriage with pretend matter-of-factness, like a couple of bad actors caught in the world's worst soap opera. . . .

Your loneliness is a tangible thing, something you become aware of all the time. This emptiness is a basement flooded with grief and you spend the first several months up to your knees in it, bailing, trying to save your house, trying not to drown. People want to help you—and they do—but you must do most of the work yourself. You find that you cannot escape the reality of loss. Rather, you must, for a period, soak in it, swim in it, absorb it even. . . .

All of this you must survive in addition to letting go, once and for all, of the life you thought you had and the future that life implied. You must learn to wear that particular shirt, and light those same candles, and cook in that casserole dish, and look out the window again at cardinals whose bright colors may affirm, on darker days, the possibilities of life, the outside chance that suffering may, one day, be suffused with sweetness and new hope.[4]

John and Paula Sandford are quoted by Rose and Mike Warnke in their book *Recovering from Divorce.* The Sandfords call divorce a far greater wounding than death, an emotional scar—ugly, unwanted, undesirable, a burden to others. Rose Warnke uses nearly an entire page to describe divorce as a horrible crime against the soul, sorrow, pain, disorienting, destructive, heartbreaking, disabling, self-pity, loss of your loved one, loss of yourself, loss of your personal identity, and feeling rejected.[5]

Other people might use such words as *freedom, relief,* or *peace.* Make your own list—as many words as you can think of to define or describe your divorce.

bitter	hateful	embarassed
painful	resentment	unwanted
long	rejection	sickening
disabling	worthlessness	helpless

When you finish your list, make a notation on your calendar to reread the list in six months. At that time, ask yourself which words you are ready to delete. Hopefully you'll be able to eliminate some terms such as disabling, self-pity, or loss of personal identity. Run a red pencil line through those words that no longer pertain to you and date them. This will help chart your healing progress.

Meeting Other Journalists

The true stories in this book are here not as bedfellows of misery, but to offer you companionship with other victims of divorce. The stories are to be used as examples or guidelines for your own writing to show you how to bring up your pain and misery in order to release it.

Along with others who wrote stories and their insights about divorce, Jane Oja wrote about the hope and healing she found from the act of writing about the pain of going through a divorce while coping with the terminal illness of her only son. (I am grateful to her and every contributor [both named and unnamed] for their experiences used in this book. Some of their writing has undergone minor editing but only to shorten it for use here. Thank you, each and every one.)

Terminal Illness, Terminal Marriage

It was in the cafeteria of the hospital that I first felt his hand on my shoulder. I'd sat there crying for an hour or more, forgetting the cold coffee sitting in front of me; oblivious to the other people chatting and eating at nearby tables; unsure if I had the strength to make my way to the elevator and back to the bedside of my gravely ill son. I was a frightened, lonely, single mom feeling abandoned by everyone I knew—even God. I'd just been told that my eleven-month-old son was dying. The hand on my shoulder both comforted and startled me.

"You look like you need someone to talk to." The kind, gentle voice came from one of the most handsome men I'd ever seen. Through the night, he sat with me in

that cafeteria, listening attentively as I poured out my sad story. It felt good to talk to a stranger about my son, Joshua, and about my fears of living without him. I was struggling as a young divorced mom, and while the medical bills were mounting, my endurance was plummeting downward.

Suddenly it occurred to me that the man sitting with me in the cafeteria might be a gift from God—the close friend I'd cried out for as I grew more desperate in my circumstances. In the ensuing months, I fell in love with Scot, only to discover, after I married him, that he had an illness of his own, an addiction to pornography and secret sexual sin.

Dealing with both a dying son and a perverted husband nearly cost me my sanity. I journaled my frustration and my prayers to God into what I called "My Book of Pain." For fourteen years, I clung to God and to the hope that both my son and my husband would be healed.

Neither happened. Instead, I found myself coping with another divorce and the enormous task of parenting Joshua and his two younger sisters Scot and I had produced together. The children were hurt and angry. How could I tell them that we'd be okay and that God would not forsake them while our house was taken away, our family car was gone, and our ability to eat was changed drastically. I told them God would heal their hurts even though I cried myself to sleep every night.

Desperately in need of a heart and kidney transplant plus a second liver transplant, my son died when he was eighteen years old. However, before he died, he spoke to audiences in churches and civic clubs in our hometown, *giving testimony about a God who gets involved in His children's lives. His glowing faith and trust in God made the front pages of the local newspaper. The community got involved in his life by raising money to pay medical bills and keep food on the table. God became my strength, my source, and my husband.*

Continually pouring the pain in my heart into the pages of my journal seemed to make room for the pain that was yet to come. Without doing that, my heart would surely have burst.

I don't have answers or excuses for my ex-husband or for those fourteen years living in a marriage full of darkness, but I've continued to trust God's plan for my life. He never fails to remind me to reach out and be available to comfort another hurting person.[6]

Perhaps as you read Jane's story, your own emotions or memories began to surface. Can you describe them? Sometimes people struggling in the aftermath of divorce feel horrendous guilt or uncertainty. Did I make a mistake? Should I have agreed to marriage counseling? Does my ex-partner know how sorry (or how angry) I am?

Make some notes below to describe your thoughts, memories, and feelings. Then, when you are ready to write, use the notes as suggested topics.

Thoughts, Memories, and Emotions!

It has been a year Since Don

told me he wanted a Divorce. But

today the pain still feels so fresh. Is it because of the 1 yr anniversary? God, I want to be on the other side of this terrible mess. Not still going thru it. Help me to get to the other side. Help me gain control of my life and start living again. Help me Lord, I'm so scared.

Maybe you'd prefer to write a shorter story. The important thing is that you write something.

Another woman who used journaling as an opportunity to put words to her feelings wrote a note to God:

> Oh Father, I am so broken. I do not feel the immensity of anger I once did but I am sickened by the effect of my husband's lack of commitment to his covenant in marriage, to You and to me and other believers. I sense he may be seeing another woman and hides in denial of Your laws. I know I can't be responsible for his relationship to You and that although I can tell him how much I can't accept divorce as a godly choice, the part of me that has been a part of him for twenty years is so sad to see him make choices that must make You cry

also. How do You watch all this and not cry thunder-storms from heaven?[7]

—— ❧ ——

For of all sad words of tongue or pen,
The saddest are these: "It might have been."
John Greenleaf Whittier[8]

—— ❧ ——

Anxiety commonly creeps in uninvited at the most incon-venient times. What does the Bible say about being anxious? If you have a concordance, it can be enlightening to look up all the Scriptures that pertain to the words *anxiety* and *anxious*. My favorite is Philippians 4:6: "Do not be anxious about anything, but in everything, by prayer and petition, with thanksgiving, present your requests to God." The reason for letting our requests be made to God is in the next verse: "And the peace of God, which transcends all understanding, will guard your hearts and your minds in Christ Jesus."

I remember, shortly after my divorce was final, I used to pray, "Lord Jesus, please guard my heart." I was lonely, and my hunger was sometimes for more than just a friendship. Our singles group at church called it "skin hungry"—when emotions cry out with desire to be held and hugged, to feel even a pat on the hand.

I missed the intoxicating aroma of British Sterling and brisk roughness of day-old whiskers, and I had to force myself to be satisfied with memories.

I had a divorced friend who once told me, "If a man would just come close enough to whisper in my ear, I'd follow him anywhere." I prayed that God would protect her heart!

Briefly describe a time when you were "skin hungry."

When I see a nice looking man who is single (I assume) and tall and has a nice smile.

It is common for divorced people to ask, "How can I feel peaceful when my heart is so full of anxiety? How will I know when God is guarding my heart and mind?"

The next two verses in Philippians (vv. 8–9) tell us how: "Finally, brothers, whatever is true, whatever is noble, whatever is right, whatever is pure, whatever is lovely, whatever is admirable—if anything is excellent or praiseworthy—think about such things. Whatever you have learned or received or heard from me, or seen in me—put it into practice. And the God of peace will be with you."

"Put it into practice" tells me that these things aren't going to come to stay just for the asking. I have to practice and practice and practice. I have to get in shape for it.

The Bible says, "The God of peace _will_ be with you." We can take that as a promise.

It works, my hurting friend. I suggest you memorize Philippians 4:8–9 and begin your practice sessions today. Write about the ways you can do that.

I need to stop looking at every man I see to see if he has a ring on his finger. But I'm

afraid I'll miss the man
God has picked out for me if
I'm not constantly looking.

Anxiety does not empty tomorrow of its sorrows, but only empties today of its strength.
Charles H. Spurgeon[9]

Men and Divorce

Most people know that the shortest verse in the Bible is "Jesus wept" (John 11:35). Yet many men find it difficult to emulate Jesus in this act of mourning the loss of someone they loved. Men have been taught the "be strong" ethic, to "be a man and don't cry." What an injustice to humanity!

I never felt more compassion and tenderness toward my husband than the first time I saw him cry. He'd always been so firm and unemotional that I was surprised to see the tears streaming down his cheeks. Yes, he was embarrassed and tried to joke them away with something like "real men don't cry."

Too late. When I saw the tears, I saw a tenderness I had never known was there. I told him, "You are more of a man today in my eyes than you have ever been before."

Too late? It's never too late to allow some painful moment to crack the hard shell that can encase the heart when pent-up emotions need to be released. Too late? For the relationship you just came out of, perhaps, but God isn't through with you yet!

Like a death, a divorce needs to be mourned. A woman is usually more communicative about her loss and therefore more likely to seek support and attend divorce support group sessions. A man, on the other hand, may feel highly private about his divorce, unwilling to share what led to the divorce. As a rule, men find it difficult to find time to mourn, and they are often fearful that they aren't doing it right.

It is not uncommon for men to use aggression, anger, and violence as grief substitutes. It is their way of masking their fear and insecurity. Or they may attempt to fool people into thinking their divorce was akin to winning the lottery. My friend Jack Hinkle told me about an on-board-ship celebration that took place when he and his wife, Julie, were on a cruise. During the evening's entertainment, everyone joined in to sing "Happy Anniversary" or "Happy Birthday" to ship guests. Then a small group in a corner began to sing "Happy Divorce to You" to a man who apparently was celebrating that milestone in his life. Jack and Julie glanced at each other across the table, both wondering if the newly divorced man was really as joyous as his friends thought he was.

Men are less likely to attempt to journal their feelings of loss, believing they can take control of them as they are accustomed to doing with other things. Fear of disclosing intimate information causes them to stuff their feelings, unaware of the negative consequences that may appear in the months and years to come. So if you are a man working through this journaling program, let me say, "Good for you!" You have taken a valuable step toward healing. You will never regret it.

— ❧ —

Journaling is the axe that chips away the pain, but you must grab the handle in both hands.[10]

— ❧ —

Responding to the Grief

Whether you are taking this journaling journey alone or with a group, I hope you'll resolve to allow the natural and normal grief responses to happen:

- Feel the mood changes.
- Cry at unexpected times.
- Talk with people when you need to.
- Don't put a lid on your pain; let it out.
- Forget about becoming your "old self" again. Expect change.
- Allow yourself sufficient time to let the grieving take its unconstrained course, and insist that others allow you this time as well.

- Don't be in a hurry to replace the mate you have just divorced, hoping the presence of someone new will ease your sorrow. When you get well, you may find that that person was only a bandage for your pain.

- Allow God to renew your faith. There is no thought God doesn't know and no act He doesn't see. There's never a muffled cry He doesn't hear nor a broken heart He can't mend.[11]

Reread the list of normal grief responses above. Write about one or two of them with which you are having difficulty right now.

- Don't put a lid on your pain
- Talk with people when you need to

How will you resolve these responses?

- Try to acknowledge when I'm not feeling the best and share that with others

When Benjamin Franklin concluded a stirring speech on the guarantees of the Constitution, a heckler shouted, "Aw, them words don't mean nothin' at all. Where's all the happiness you say it guarantees us?"

Franklin smiled and replied, "My friend, the Constitution only guarantees the American people the right to pursue happiness; you have to catch it yourself."[12]

So it is with this journaling program. You have in your hands a book of guidelines for healing, but you have to "catch it" yourself. Rolling away the stone in front of your own sepulchre is no easy task; it takes choosing. I urge you to place your shoulder against the rock.[13]

The pains, the heartaches, the losses of our lives can become the altar on which we offer up to God all the things that keep us relying on our own strength.

Verdell Davis[14]

Some things I'm thinking, feeling, wishing, hoping, doing:

Date: 2/11/03 — I'm trying to come to grips with the idea of the 1 yr anniversary of the time Don told me he wanted a divorce. 1 yr. I wish I was further in the healing process. I want to get on with my life. I want to get a job. I want my children to quit hurting. I want to start dating again. Nothing serious. I want a house of my own. Lord, come with me on this journey of healing.

Responses to Divorce Grief

— ❧ —

The weathercock on the church spire, though made of iron, would soon be broken by the storm-wind if it . . . did not understand the noble art of turning to every wind.

Heinrich Heine

— ❧ —

Congratulations!

Good for you for being willing to tackle chapter 2. Let me reassure you, it will become easier as you work through the maze of your divorce by journaling. Don't let your apprehension get in the way of participating and benefiting from this program. If you feel pain as you attempt this writing, it's because your pain is being released. You are not stuffing it but setting it free!

When victims of divorce become depressed and weary, they sometimes forget that God wants to be a source of comfort. It is difficult to maintain fellowship with Him while sinking in despair. The Bible is full of promises that can bring hope.

> For the LORD comforts his people and will have compassion on his afflicted ones.
>
> Isaiah 49:13b

> God has said, "Never will I leave you; never will I forsake you."
>
> Hebrews 13:5b

Remember God's promises as you write in your journal.

There are no right or wrong topics, no right or wrong emotions, no right or wrong ways to record your journey through the process of your divorce. There is value in putting your thoughts on paper in that you will be able to go back and read what you wrote in these early sessions and see the progress you have made.

Ponder on those things that have happened in your life since you became "single again." Are you paying child support for children you no longer come home to? Are you holding down a job for the first time in many years? On the following lines, make a list or write a story describing the changes and how they have affected your life.

I no longer have a home of my own.
I had to quit my job. Perfect part-time job.
Sell my house- that I help build
I can no longer be the stay
 at home Mom that I wanted
 to be.
Financially I'm hurting
Paying for Counselling for Kelsey
 because of what Don did?!
Single Mom- making decisions
 on my own
The Kids have to get use to the not
 being able to buy things when
 they want them. (me too)

Identifying My Own Responses to Divorce

The concept of "stages of grief" was popularized in 1969 with the publication of Elizabeth Kubler-Ross's book, *On Death and Dying.*[1] In the same way, the grief of divorce may seem to progress in stages. However, I have come to understand how each person's grief passage is uniquely his or her own, not proceeding in any order or stage; therefore I prefer to call these experiences "responses."

1. We are on mental, physical, and spiritual overload. It becomes difficult to make wise decisions as we feel pushed to act before we are ready. The mind seems to shut down, the body feels total exhaustion, and the spirit perceives abandonment. We might wonder if we are going crazy. Read Matthew 11:28— God's promise for overload.

2. We express emotion in many ways. Emotional release comes as the finality of the divorce begins to be realized. We are torn between the dreadful loss of a dream and our desires that demand justice and fairness. Often, without warning, emotional release is expressed as tears, angry outbursts, overeating, or drinking. We try to fill the void created by the divorce with criticism directed toward the person whom we perceive has hurt us deeply.

"He who guards his lips guards his life, but he who speaks rashly will come to ruin" (Prov. 13:3).

3. We feel depressed and lonely, even though we often wanted out of the relationship. It is as if God is no longer in His heaven, as if God does not care. During these times of utter depression, we sometimes wonder if God really knows what is going on in our lives.

"My tears have been my food day and night, while men say to me all day long, 'Where is your God?' I say to God my Rock, 'Why have you forgotten me?'" (Ps. 42:3, 9a).

4. *We may experience physical symptoms of distress.* Some people are ill because of unresolved issues. No amount of medication will significantly change the need to acknowledge and begin to reconcile the losses brought about by divorce.

"Be merciful to me, O LORD, for I am in distress; my eyes grow weak with sorrow, my soul and my body with grief" (Ps. 31:9).

5. *We may become panicky and want to run away.* Even when we try to get our mind off the subject, we can think of nothing but the divorce. Resolving property settlements, unfaithfulness, or noncommunication may become so all-consuming that we no longer can contribute to any solutions. Feeling the hopelessness of it all, we try to separate ourselves from the divorce physically and emotionally.

"Answer me when I call to you, O my righteous God. Give me relief from my distress; be merciful to me and hear my prayer" (Ps. 4:1).

6. *We feel a sense of guilt about the divorce.* Real and normal is the guilt that accompanies divorce: guilt that we couldn't hold the marriage together, guilt for mistakes we made, guilt that we married the wrong person, guilt because we know God hates divorce. Neurotic guilt is feeling guilty out of proportion to our own real involvement in the breakdown of the marriage. Praying, "Create in me a pure heart, O God, and renew a steadfast spirit within me" (Ps. 51:10) can bring a remarkable sense of relief.

7. *We are filled with anger, resentment, and feelings of rejection.* These feelings are normal for even the most devout person. However, in confession, we must admit our inability

to cope and ask God for strength to work through the feelings and face the truth.

"O LORD, how many are my foes! How many rise up against me! Many are saying of me, 'God will not deliver him.' But you are a shield around me, O LORD; you bestow glory on me and lift up my head" (Ps. 3:1–3).

8. *We resist making a new life for ourselves.* For many, divorce means living alone for the first time because they married soon after getting out of school. We desire someone to take care of us. It is possible to keep the pain and anger alive by refusing to learn new things.

"He who began a good work in you will carry it on to completion until the day of Christ Jesus" (Phil. 1:6b).

9. *Gradually hope comes through.* We discover that we can smile or laugh again. There dawns a consciousness that others also have problems. We need to acknowledge that our new chance at life is a gift from God.

"Every good and perfect gift is from above, coming down from the Father of the heavenly lights, who does not change like shifting shadows" (James 1:17).

10. *We struggle to see value in our plight.* When we go through any significant grief experience, we come out of it as different people. How we respond will make us either stronger or weaker—healthier in spirit or sicker. Many develop a deeper faith in God as a result of their divorce experience.

"Consider it pure joy, my brothers, whenever you face trials of many kinds, because you know that the testing of your faith develops perseverance. Perseverance must finish its work so that you may be mature and complete, not lacking anything" (James 1:2–4).

The above list of responses to divorce grief may help you understand some of your feelings. It is possible that you won't go through all these experiences, and, even as the order varies, some responses may return again and again.

After reading the list, try to identify those responses you have already experienced. Write about the one you feel you are in now. What is helping you?

Remember, your writing is best done when you are alone at home, in your favorite chair, or in the stillness of the night when you have trouble sleeping.

Sometimes finding a quiet place in the park or sitting by a babbling brook might help you get in touch with your feelings.

8 - resist making a new life

— ❧ —

Perhaps because I have asked so many questions
and sought so many answers,
I have at least come to know enough about God that
when I doubt His love, I hold to His wisdom.
When I can't understand His justice,
I cling to His mercies.
When I wonder about His faithfulness,
I cherish His grace.
When I fear his sovereignty, I bow to His holiness.
And in that my heart can rest.
                                     Verdell Davis[2]

— ❧ —

It is important to keep nurturing a positive attitude. Our spiritual nature cannot feed on negatives. *The person who is constantly reciting the faults of another will never see his own.* He is like a man running a race looking back over his shoulder. It is important to realize that life will never be the same again, but there is much in life that can be affirmed.

How's your attitude? _____*Okay*_____

What would you like to change about your attitude, and how can you do that?

_____*Stop joking about Don & amy*_____

At the time of great pain or deep sorrow, people who have a mature faith give evidence of an uncommon relationship with God. And they demonstrate an uncommon inner sense of strength and poise that grows out of the *confidence that such a relationship with God can never be taken away from them.* With that assurance they find themselves able to adjust to any earthly loss. They still have God on whom to rely. It makes an amazing difference in the quality of the divorce experience.

New interests, new friendships, and new life are the healing banquet prepared just for survivors. But no one will fill your plate; you must do that for yourself.

— ❧ —

*Tomorrow has two handles: the handle of fear
and the handle of faith. You can take hold of
it by either handle.*

Author unknown[3]

— ❧ —

Learning the Things I Really Didn't Want to Know

There are stabs of pain the divorced endure that the widowed do not:

- You've been told the name of the woman (or man) seen with your ex-mate; or of the good fortune of a vacation or increase in pay for the one you divorced.

- The former spouse has filed papers to take your children out of state to live.

- Child support or alimony checks have stopped.

- People in your church are shunning you because you are divorced.

- Your own parents are blaming you for the divorce.

The following blanks provide a place to pour out all of the injustices that plague you. Let go of the pieces of the puzzle that no longer fit. Saw off the infected branches of your bitterness tree. Scrape loose the glue that binds you to that person. Pour all of those grievances into a list or story, and if there are too many to record here, get as many additional pieces of paper as you need, and don't stop until you feel cleansed.

~ Don left me for a woman 10 yrs. younger with no kids

~ He lived in our home we built together, with her.

~ When my kids visit their Dad, she
  is living there with him, sleeping w/him
~ He makes the Decision to leave
  but I don't have any rights, he does
~ Kelsey needs counseling but he won't pay
~ I lost family, my in-laws
~ Don is marrying Amy soon
~ He gets to claim the kids for tax purposes

If you need to set fire to those papers saturated in pain and
anger, or tear them into bits to be carried away by the wind, you
can do that. It is helpful to do something physical when you
have finished your list even if it is only to flush shredded pieces
down the toilet. When you say good-bye to all the inequities
you wrote about, you must tell them they are no longer welcome in your house, your mind, or your heart.

— ❧ —

There is no torment like the inner torment of
an unforgiving spirit. It refuses to be soothed, it
refusees to be healed, it refuses to forget. . . .
You cannot nurture the bitterness plant and
at the same time keep it concealed. The bitter
root bears bitter fruit.
                                      Charles Swindoll[4]

— ❧ —

Definable Feelings and Fears

In an attempt to face her feelings and fears, Joyce Lee wrote:

> *Resting in you, Lord, is not a natural thing for me. Yet, I've heard you say you would make the paths straight and I have heard you say knock and you will answer. I rise every morning and read your Word that says you will fight on my behalf. This morning I read how I must obey you, with my heart, my will, my mind, my body, my finances and my future. . . . Please let me read about the comfort and peace of the Holy Spirit. This is a very uncertain time. I wonder sometimes if you really know how much more I can take. Please hear my heart, Lord.[5]*

It is sometimes difficult to be totally honest with God even though He knows all of our thoughts and feelings and fears. It is also difficult to tell God you are disappointed in Him (or angry at Him) for not rescuing your troubled marriage or changing your spouse like you asked Him to do. Sometimes we need to be reminded that God can handle our honesty.

He is also wise enough to know which feelings come from our heart and which ones are simply from our pain. Write your feelings down and then talk to Him about them.

My kids are gone this weekend with their Dad. I worry when their gone. How are they doing? How are their hearts. What sin are they seeing. Why does this have to be so hard & unfair. I didn't want this. Why do I pay the pain?

35

Feelings

Feelings deal with the logic of the heart. Feelings may be deeply profound or just a gut reaction to a situation. Feelings control your emotional life, sentiments, impressions, hunches, passion, fury, gusto, and sometimes feelings control your reactions or responses to everything around you.

Divorce damages feelings. The results can be hostility, conflict, and even hard-heartedness. See if you can find a Scripture in the Bible that warns us about such feelings.

Eph. 5:31 - Get rid of all bitterness,
rage + anger, brawling and slander
along with every form of malice

How does that Scripture pertain to you?

I need to get rid of my malice
towards Don

Make a list of other feelings you need to deal with such as disappointment, anger, guilt, or rejection.

anger, disappointment,
frustration, unfair
abandonment, fear

Don't forget the positive feelings you are having such as relief, release, joy, a chance for a new future.

release, chance of a new future

excitement

Then write about feelings: How and when did you begin to feel the words you listed? What have you done to cope with them, or what will you do?

2-17-04

I felt most of the bad feelings from day 1. The positive feelings are coming everday. Some days the bad feelings are fresh & on the surface. Other days they are bearable.

Be sure to date your journalings so that as your feelings and emotions change, you'll be able to document your progress.

It may be difficult to accomplish complete control over your negative feelings all at once. Take some time every day to let the Scriptures nourish your thirsting soul. Even with the Word of God guiding your life, it is slow work to uproot that which has influenced your past and replant the faith that enables you to say, "All things have become new." Don't try to hurry, but take time to gather up armfuls of God's good gifts along the way.

*The hands that created the exquisite geometry
of the snowflake and painted the beautiful bell
of the lily . . . those hands that were pierced
on the cross of Calvary will take hold of our
tangled lives and make them whole again!*

Henry Gariepy[6]

Fears

Fear is to be expected in a fallen world. What is not expected is for God's people to experience fear. Like a demon who has taken up residency on the bedpost, fear announces his presence at those times when we have worn thin the desire or energy to combat him. In the middle of the night he begins his taunting questions:

- "Aren't you afraid of living alone?"
- "Who would know or care if something happened to you?"
- "Don't you know your best, most productive years are over?"
- "How will you manage now? The kids need both a mommy and daddy. Aren't you cheating them?"
- "Aren't you afraid of becoming selfish and lonely with no friends and family?"
- "Who will supply your needs?"

And the bedpost demon continues to mock your efforts and deplete your strength. What does he say to you? List your fears, and then write about the one that troubles you the most.

living alone, raising the kids without a dad, supporting them① I gave up my career for the kids to be a stay at home mom. Now I don't have experience to get a good job.

When the demon asked, "Who will supply your needs?" what came to your mind? God said He "will meet all your needs according to his glorious riches in Christ Jesus" (Phil. 4:19). Can you count on that?

Yes, God will supply all my needs & my kids needs also.

The Bible also says:

For God hath not given us the spirit of fear; but of power, and of love, and of a sound mind.

2 Timothy 1:7 KJV

So we say with confidence, "The Lord is my helper, I will not be afraid. What can man do to me?"

Hebrews 13:6

One journaler wrote: "My devotions today remind me to abolish fear knowing I can be confident in the Lord's guidance and protection. I am also reminded to seek the fellowship of a Christian small group."

For me, devotions early in the morning help set the pace for the day. Small group fellowship reminds me I am not alone. What steps are you taking to abolish your fears?

Trying to find a Divorce support group. Devotions in the morning with prayer time. Talking to people about my fears.

I want to encourage you to make this your own personal prayer:

> *Forgive me, Lord, for those moments of fear, those times when I don't lift all my burdens from my shoulders to yours . . . knowing you will still have arms to embrace me and make me secure.[7] Please, Lord, continue the work you have begun in me. Show me when I am ready to turn another page in this book and therefore another page in my life. Amen.*

Some things I'm thinking, feeling, wishing, hoping, doing:

Date: 2-18-04 - I met with Pastor Don Bishop today. I needed to get some advice about what to do about Don's anger and violence with the kids. I also explained to him my feelings of wanting Don to die. I want him dead so the kids won't have to suffer. I know its wrong. He said I was at this point because I've lost hope that Don can change. Pastor Don said that wishing him dead was not the answer, but was very normal. He said to keep confessing it to God. "Dear God, I hate Don + want him to die so my kids don't have to suffer any longer. Please take these feelings and help me."

41

Don got so mad at the kids this last weekend. Kelsey told me how he got so mad because they asked for something from WalMart. He stopped the truck, started hitting things in the truck and yelling at them. Kelsey wanted out of the truck but Don told Blake to lock the doors. Kelsey told Don he needed help with his anger and should go to counseling. He said he couldn't afford it. After he just showed Kelsey a 47" plasma TV he was buying. Kelsey started crying and said she wanted to go home. Don threw the cell phone at her and told her to call me. Don was swearing very badly. Blake was crying. They were both so scared. Blake said he yells at them all the time. Blake doesn't want to go for a whole weekend. He wants just 1 day. Kelsey said the next day after a fight he is really nice to them. Typical of an abuser. God help me make the right decision about what I need to do about Don & his anger

Facing Firsts

*Neither a wise man nor a brave man lies
down on the tracks of history to wait for the
train of the future to run over him.*

Dwight D. Eisenhower

Facing Firsts

Some people find it painful to keep hearing how they are now an "X"—an ex-wife or ex-husband. It is like the "X" is crossing out who you were, making the divorced feel like they have been erased. When did someone first call you an "X," and how did it sound and feel?

I haven't had someone call me that but part of me would be ashamed.

First times can be empowering or debilitating, depending upon your outlook. First-time things for you right now might include mowing the lawn, going to a laundromat, eating in a restaurant alone, or going for an outing with the kids on a Sunday afternoon without the companionship that made you the other half of "a couple." Some people feel set free to try things for the first time, while others struggle to cope.

Note some of your firsts since your marriage was dissolved.

First oil change in the car that was my responsibility:

Randy takes my van for me

First experience at the laundromat:

don't have to do

First time to try to get credit since I've been single again:

haven't yet

Other firsts:

Going to church without Dan or the kids, alone. It's very hard and still is.

How do these things differ from when you were married?

I had someone to share the experience of worship with. Someone to sit with not be alone.

As you consider your new singleness, you'll find many "firsts" and "lasts" that will have an impact on your life, possibly bringing increased sorrow or confusion: the first holiday as a broken family, your birthday without flowers or dinner out, and especially spending your wedding anniversary alone. In the space below, write about one "first" you've already experienced. Include how you felt when it happened. If you could do it over, how would you handle it differently?

The Christmas holidays. I did better than I had imagined. I spent a lot of money on the kids trying to make up for Dad being gone. After the holiday is when the depression set in.

Now write about one or more "firsts" that you look forward to: A vacation with a friend? A quiet house without the TV on? Getting your bills paid? A weekend retreat?

Paying bills & knowing exactly how much money I have. Quiet weekends

Since your divorce, how have your responsibilities changed?

Not too much. I did most of the things I'm doing now when we were married

You now may have to tackle things your former spouse always handled. For example, Greg felt angry at his wife for not being there to help him do the taxes. It was so foreign to him. Name a difficult chore you will now face. *Car maintenance?*

Who will help you? *Randy*

Make a list of your support team.

Family *Randy, Rhonda, my parents and sisters*

Friends _Jane, Kim, Don & Kris Bishop_

Club or place of employment _____

Pastor, priest, or others at your church or synagogue _____

Don Bishop

Doctor/counselor _____

Pets _Abby_

Others _Christ, my bible, Kelsey counselor, my lawyer_

Refer to this list when you are feeling alone and think no one cares.

The following prayer written by Ruth Bell Graham will also remind you that you are not alone.

Lord, when my soul is weary
and my heart is tired and sore,
and I have that failing feeling
that I can't take any more;
then let me know the freshening
found in simple, childlike prayer,
when the kneeling soul knows surely
that a listening Lord is there.[1]

Facing Reality

What would you say about facing reality? It stinks? Perhaps that is what this man was trying to say:

> *Yuk! What smells? I staggered from my bed into the kitchen early one Saturday morning. The boys were still asleep and I longed for some time by myself to read, to pray, to listen to the stillness of my own heart. My nose led me to piles of broken pieces, bitten pieces, smelly chunks of last nights pizza on the table, on the counter-top, and in the sink. This is just one more thing that has changed. Their mother would never have gone to bed leaving such a smelly mess in the house. I miss her tidiness. I miss her. Divorce smells like leftover pizza.*[2]

The reality of divorce changes peoples lives. It ravages families. It is denounced from the pulpit. It dissolves lifelong friendships. It institutes financial ruin. The statistics include victims in the church—good, upstanding, honest, God-fearing members of every church. They are wounded people, bewildered and lost, who need spiritual healing and transformation to be able to function in the church again.

Divorced people sit in the lonely corners of the church because the lonely corners in their heart direct them there. How do the people of your church respond to you as a divorced person?

Some respond with love, concern and caring. Like Jane & Phil, Kris, Gloria. But others who don't know me, they don't seem to want to get to know me.

List the things you wish were different in your church's overall attitude about divorce.

More openness
a divorce support group

List the benefits your church offers for the divorced.

acceptance

People who have traveled the

road before.

Is there a divorce support group in your church? Does there need to be?

No, there isn't, they are trying

to put one together.

Facing Forgiveness

Some of you who are participating in this journaling program have suffered many wounds that fester anew at every mention of his or her name. Unfortunately, the result of these injuries can lead to a severe bondage to unforgiveness. As you name your wounds, what would you write about them? For instance, Joyce wrote,

> *David asked about all the years I didn't work and I strongly reminded him that, in my eyes, I have never stopped working since the day we were married. However, for ten years, I didn't get paid.*
>
> *I think I have reached my capacity of all this garbage. I refuse to be beaten up by the negativity, lack of*

provisional and financial responsibility, and the continual blame.[3]

Now name your wound. Perhaps it was being lied to or being physically injured or being dumped for another person. List more than one if you wish.

The one that hurts the most is the fact that his anger & outbursts are hurting the kids & scaring them.

Naming your wounds gives opportunity to hold them before the Lord and ask, "Do I need to work on this?" or "Is this a lie?"

There is a good chance here that you are asking yourself, "How can I ever forgive that?" Before you go any further, try to define the word *forgiveness*. Forgiveness is . . .

not wanting revenge on another person for a wrong they have committed

Dr. Charles Stanley defines *forgiveness* as "the act of setting someone free from an obligation to you that is a result of a wrong done against you."[4]

Forgiveness does not say, "You will get over it in time." It is not saying, "It didn't matter." Forgiveness does not happen by stifling your feelings about the circumstances that brought the pain. Forgiveness is an act, something that requires an effort on your part. Forgiveness is God's desire for you no matter how much someone has wronged you.

Before you can deal with your unforgiveness issues, it would be wise to look at God's perspective on unforgiveness. To help see it more clearly, take a moment to pray for clarification and the capability to resolve things in the same way God does. Ask Him to reveal what He desires for you. Write out your prayer if you wish.

Dear Lord Help me to forgive Don completely and not want him dead for what he's done Lord. please take this & show me how to handle it.

Date prayed: __2-19-04__ Hopefully someday you will come back to this page in this book and enter: Date prayer was answered: _____!

God's perspective on forgiveness seems pretty clear as we read Scripture.

> *Bear with each other and forgive whatever grievances you may have against one another. Forgive as the Lord forgave you.*
>
> Colossians 3:13

> *And when you stand praying, if you hold anything against anyone, forgive him, so that your Father in heaven may forgive you your sins.*
>
> Mark 11:25

List some other verses about forgiveness that you are familiar with.

> Matt 18: 21-22 - forgiving seven times seventy-seven.
>
> Luke 23:34 - Father forgive them for they do not know what they are doing.

Write about what those verses are saying to you personally.

> Matt - I doesn't matter what or how many times Don hurts the kids, I need to forgive him.
>
> Luke - Jesus forgave those who were killing him, I need to forgive Don

For me, forgiveness is an act of the will—a decision to release negative thoughts of bitterness and resentment. I can refuse to forgive and stay miserable and unhappy because someone sinned against me, or I can let go and let God judge them. Letting God deal with each wound frees me to move away from the unhappy portion of my life to seek His plans for my future life.

Unfortunately, forgiving does not always include forgetting. In an article for the *Baltimore Sun*, reporter Susan Reimer wrote about forgiveness as an act of healing the heart and mind: "Its meaning and its method can be as elusive as the moment when it is felt. It is not some cheap grace that we claim for ourselves or offer to another. We know that forgiving is not excusing, condoning, pretending, ignoring or suppressing."[5]

Reimer told about a woman named Anna.

Anna's husband of 25 years simply said he didn't love her anymore. "That hurt more than anything, . . . " she said. "It represents total rejection."

She asked him to stay for six months while she found her footings, found a job. He did. During their last months together, Anna . . . realized that she could not build a future on hating him. Neither she nor her children would survive if they fed on that kind of poison. "I also recognize that there were things in our marriage that were not good. In forgiving him, I have to recognize my own faults.

"There is a huge difference in how I feel now. The true feeling of forgiving is definitely there. I have prayed, and I have a deeper spiritual understanding of who God is, a true feeling of peace and comfort. I know that I am still a good person. And there is a sense of freedom. It is so liberating.

"The anxiousness and depression are gone. There are still plenty of tears, but they are tears of healing. I'm not stuck. . . ."

Christ taught his followers that forgiveness is a way of life. He demonstrated it fully when He asked God from the cross to forgive his crucifiers. . . . He wasn't just talking about our country's enemies or the criminal who violates us. He was talking about . . . the parent who wounds with words, the sibling who turns his back, . . . the spouse who betrays.[6]

Shared Parenting

This journaling program has been compiled to help you cope with your personal losses, not the losses of others; therefore we will touch only lightly on the topic of children. The lessons and processing you are doing will hopefully help you to be able to reach stability and enjoyment of life again, which will certainly also benefit your children. The way in which you do that will affect their belief that they can someday be in a solid, committed Christian marriage even though their parents divorced.

Like many parents who go through divorce, one parent may feel the need to shelter the children, believing she or he is the better parent. However, there are some parents who can successfully parent their children together even after a divorce.

Shared parenting happens only when two parents are willing to put aside their marriage obstacles and work through issues exclusively regarding the children. It not only helps the children feel comfortable with having two parents in two different households, it also helps grandparents continue a relationship with the children.

When couples have no children, pets have been known to become a custody issue. Or when a spouse moves to an apartment where dogs are prohibited, she or he may demand visiting rights while the one in custody demands compensation for the food and medical expenses of a "shared" pet. For all the people involved, whether sharing the children or an animal, godly principles of tolerance, patience, forgiveness, and prayer are a must.

Is shared parenting an option for you?

Why or why not?

It is really hard right now because Communicating with Don is nearly impossible with his anger & out bursts

Write out your thoughts about ways to help the children adjust to shared parenting.

I want to get to the point where I can trust Dons judgement as a parent. I fear for my kids when they are with him. I don't want that anymore

Are there some ways you have already tried shared parenting that were or were not successful?

Allmost all dealings with Don were unsuccessful. I pretty much make the decisions. He has no desire to and can't.

How can you use the concept of shared parenting when one of the parents has abandoned the family? Have you tried filling the gaps with a grandparent or trading time slots with another family that has a parent gap? Write your thoughts about this.

Randy & Rhonda feel in the gaps.
I feel Don has abandoned Kelsey &
Blake. But Randy is a good
male role model.

Write out some ways you can help your children feel secure while still releasing them to God and, if appropriate, to the other parent. Pray for God's guidance before you write.

Praying with them before they
go with their Dad- Or will this
frighten them? In our evening prayers
before they go w/ him I pray for
safety & that they will enjoy their time.
I think this might be less scarey.

Read the following prayer, and then ask yourself if this is one you should be praying:

Sometimes, Lord, I wonder what is wrong with me that I am drowning in this sea of disappointment and sad experiences. Help me to refuse to give in to the depression that offers to swamp me and drag me under.

And Lord, help me not to overlook those good qualities in the children's father [or mother]. May I never be responsible for teaching bitterness, hate, or rejection. At the same time, Lord, help me to recognize my own good qualities as well as my weaknesses and shortcomings during this time when my heart cries out to be comforted and encouraged.

Thank You that You have blessed each of us as a unique and precious individual in Your sight.

Amen.

My Brag Page

If you have children, write a pageful about them. Include their ages, dates of birth, names, funny characteristics, grades, hobbies, and that special quality you love about each one.

Kelsey - 14, 8-27-89 - She's bright, beautiful, outgoing, kind, I feel She's going to do or be something great when she grows up. Right now, I am so proud of her grades. She will be receiving an Academic letter & award for her 4.3 grade average for 2 Qtrs. I'm proud she made the Volleyball team. I'm proud of her piano. She is just so beautiful inside and out. She's funny, brave & courageous

Blake - 8 - (9.30.95) - He is so tender hearted, smart, helpful, loving, I'm proud of how he helps others in school and at home. He loves sports - especially soccer - He made 2 goals at the last tournament he played in. He picks really good friends. He is very close to my heart. I'm so proud of him in everything.

— ❧ —

Do not fear, for I am with you,
do not be afraid, for I am your God;
I will strengthen you,
I will help you, I will uphold you
with my victorious right hand.
Isaiah 41:10 NRSV

— ❧ —

Some things I'm thinking, feeling, wishing, hoping, doing:

Date: 2-24-04 - A few weeks ago, I felt like I had hit another wall. I felt as tho I was not as close to God, I felt like something was in the way. It was around the time that the kids had a very hard weekend with their Dad. Anyway I talked with Pastor Don about how I was feeling and about the hatred I had for Don & wanting him dead. Pastor Don told me to confess it to God in a way that said "This is how I'm feeling God. I give it to you, help me with it." I have been praying this & I feel as if a wall has fallen down. I feel closer to God. I'm so glad I went to see Pastor Don. I thought confessing my feelings to God meant that

I was sorry for them. And at that time I wasn't sorry that I felt I wanted Don dead. I felt that my anger was justified because Don had & is hurting the birds. Pastor Don said that was what all sin is. A justified response. As I confessed to God my feelings & asked him to help me with these feelings, I've felt a peace. I still get angry at God & Don but I keep confessing it to God. I've seen Gods blessings in the past weeks. The next time I feel far away from God, I need to remember to confess to him and ask him to show me my sin, and listen, really listen.

Dear Ex

— ❧ —

*A word aptly spoken is like apples of
gold in settings of silver.*

Proverbs 25:11

— ❧ —

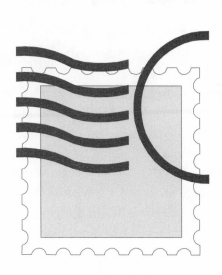

Dear Ex

As you begin session four, stop to think and write about how far you've come in your notebook and in your recovery.

I feel like come a long way. I purchased this book to help me get thru this terrible time & it is helping. It's easier to journal when questions are asked, then to write on a blank piece of paper. I feel my heart healing.

Probably much to your chagrin, this session is about letter writing. It will be your last chance in this workbook to say something to or about the person you are divorcing (or are already divorced from) as we will begin to examine the new person you are becoming in the next chapter.

There may be times you struggle to fight off an intense longing to communicate with your ex-spouse. You decide not to do it because it may expose your feelings of loneliness or because you are wanting to lash out from your pain. Whatever the reason, that urge for contact can often be filled by means of letter writing. It is a safe way to discharge anger that might be directed at your former mate because after the letter "cools," you may decide to toss it.

Remember, writing can help diminish guilt, clarify your thoughts, and be a more comfortable way to unload the feelings that you are not willing to share with another human being.

Here are some ideas to start your letter writing:

- ❧ What I miss most about being married
- ❧ What I wish I'd said—or hadn't said
- ❧ What I've had the hardest time dealing with
- ❧ What I'd like to ask my ex if we could talk

List some of your own ideas of topics for letter writing.

Does he regret what he's done?

Is Amy everything he needed?

The hardest thing has been the kids' pain

Why is he so angry & depressed

Why did he cut himself off of everyone

• Not being married is easier than I

thought it would be.

— ❧ —

Suppression leads to momentary relief
and permanent pain. Feeling your
experience leads to momentary pain
and permanent relief.
Chinese proverb[1]

— ❧ —

I was hurt and confused when I wrote this letter to my husband:

Dear Dick:

I cried a lot again yesterday and I was angry at myself for crying so much. Then the mail came and an article in a new magazine caught my eye. It was called, "Lonely Housewives."

They are the women married to good, hard-working, likable men. The men's lives are fulfilled by their jobs, by friends who fish, hunt and attend sport events, and by a wife who cares for his every need. She cooks, cleans, entertains, cares for the children, does all the shopping, and inquires about his job, his day, his health and his needs.

The article said a man gets so comfortable and self-satisfied that he doesn't even think his wife has any needs. He knows nothing about her desires, thoughts, or problems. He is happy so why shouldn't she be?

That's what happened to us, Dick.

I want you to know I am angry that we didn't fight for our marriage. I am hurt and frustrated that you couldn't or wouldn't try to see my needs as a woman.

The magazine article listed ways to deal with anger. They were *suppression*, *expression* and *confession*.

Well, I've been *suppressing* my feelings long enough. That's why I have colitis and headaches. And I don't know how to do the *expression*. I'm not good at blowing up, yelling and saying the unkind things I really would like to say.

That leaves me only *confession*. I confess I am angry with you. I have no plans and no future, only deep pain for the marriage that wouldn't heal itself; the marriage that got buried alive. I confess to God that I didn't try to salvage it either. I've asked Him to forgive me. I really hope you will, too. I know I also need to forgive myself.

The time has come for me to take responsibility for my own feelings, my own life and let go of you. I don't want to do that but I must. You probably will never see this letter and that's fine because I feel better for having written it.

Barbara[2]

For letters you want to write and actually send, use a separate piece of paper instead of writing in your book.

Before you begin your letter, ask yourself this question: "If I knew this was the last communication I would ever have with my ex-spouse, what would I want to say?"

Dear __Don_____ Date __2-27-04__

Well, it's been over a year since you left me & the kids. Did you find what you were looking for? Was it worth all the pain that you've caused the kids? Why are you so angry and Depressed? I wish you would go and get some help. I know we will never be together again & I'm ok with that. But please get some help so you can stop hurting the kids.

Lisa

What will you do with your letter?

I can't send it. Don is not in his right mind. I'm afraid he'd get angry and take it out on the kids.

Before you make any final decision as to the disposition of your letter, hold it in your hand and offer it up to the God of beginnings and endings. Ask Him to help you bid farewell to this relationship that has brought you so much pain and grief. Don't hurry this process, but do be sure your letter doesn't get into the hands of someone you don't want to share it with.

If you plan to send it to the person you've addressed, I suggest you let it mellow. Put it away in a safe place and don't look at it again for forty-eight hours. When you retrieve it, pretend you have never seen it before—try to read it with "new eyes."

Slowly dissect each line, then each paragraph. Would you be comfortable reading your letter aloud in the presence of both the addressee and the Lord?

Yes

Why or why not?

Because I asked honest questions with no malice and request him to get help.

Are you sending the letter to get a response or just to give information?

It would be nice to get answers to the questions but I don't think Don even knows.

Was there some element of satisfaction in just writing the letter?

Not really

If you mail the letter, how will you cope with a response other than the one you hope for—or the feelings of rejection that may come with no response at all?

You may wish to carefully, slowly tear the letter into small pieces as a sign of the tear in the relationship. Let the wind carry the pieces high into the sky.

Or you may want to reread the letter by candlelight, then ignite it on the candle flame as you say good-bye to the pain and hello to a new life.

Are there others who would appreciate a letter from you?

- Your attorney
- Your children and your parents
- A family who stuck by you
- A pastor who counseled you
- The friend you leaned on and received encouragement from
- Others

Damaged Dreams and Difficult Decisions

They go together. Damaged dreams bring about difficult decisions, and sometimes it is the decisions that damage the dreams. One of my dreams since grade school was to be a writer. This goal seemed hampered by the man I married when he'd say, "You've got plenty to do at home taking care of the family without writing. Why can't you just be satisfied?" My overachieving personality felt cheated out of an outlet for my restless creativity.

Occasionally, I found other ways to use my gifts. I wrote a column for the local newspaper for nearly a year, but I never heard my husband say, "That's good" or "I'm proud of you." I wanted encouragement.

I needed reassurance when I was the PTA president, full of hopes and plans for a united parents' association interacting like family with the future of our children as our overall cause. It embarrassed my husband for me to be up on the platform in front instead of in the seat beside him in the audience.

I quit. My dreams all seemed to be troublemakers, and finally I learned to stop dreaming. I changed. Somewhere on the inside of this outgoing, fun-loving woman, fear of displeasing my mate became like a weight cemented to my heart. My dreams dried up like yard leaves, and life became meaningless.

I learned the benefit of wearing masks. I became so comfortable wearing my masks that I'd forget which face was real and which one was fake. My restless creativity taunted me when I observed others living out their dreams, and that's when the ugly head of jealousy would sneer and hiss at me and tell me I had no value.

Your Dreams

Some of you had a dream like living happily ever after or having more children or growing old together. Write about your dream . . . the one you had to give up because life didn't turn out the way you planned.

My dream of being a stay at home Mom. I would be available for my kids before + after school. and During the summer.

What is keeping you from pursuing that dream now?

Financial reasons

Because of damaged dreams, you've been (or still are) having to make some difficult decisions. Did you have to decide to sell that new home to provide for a division of assets? Or was your employment requiring some difficult decisions? If one child wants to live with Dad and another with Mom, that poses a difficult, heartbreaking, dream-damaging decision. Who can make such difficult decisions? Can you? Can God?

Its so hard to make tough decisions. Like if I should take a job or not. I just keep praying about it.

Harold Kushner addressed this question in his book *When Bad Things Happen to Good People*: "Where do you get the strength to go on when you have used up all of your own strength? Where do you turn for patience when you have run out of patience, when you have been more patient for more years than anyone should be asked to be, and the end is nowhere in sight? I believe that God gives us strength and patience and hope, renewing our spiritual resources when they run dry."[3]

— ❦ —

Those who hope in the LORD
will renew their strength.
They will soar on wings like eagles;
they will run and not grow weary,
they will walk and not be faint.

Isaiah 40:31

— ❦ —

Is There a Glue That Can Repair the Broken Pieces of Your Marriage?

Perhaps you've asked *Why?* and *How?* over and over as I did during that sorrowful, frozen period of my life. I often laid awake for hours at night reflecting on my motives, his motives; my disappointments, his disappointments; my future, his future. *Why did it have to come to this?* My heart was ripped down the middle. One half was light and free, full of my anticipated future and dreams. The other half longed to be best friends with the man I was once married to.

I thought about what it was that attracted me to him in the first place and began to make a list. He was generous, ambitious, fun-loving . . . and my list grew. Make your own list on the lines below.

before marriage   *during marriage*

tall	love for the Lord	
handsome	Good Father	
Popular	always helped people	

Do some of these attributes still exist? Is there a tiny flame flickering for another chance? This book would do you an injustice if it did not ask, *Have you ever considered reconciliation?*

No, Don has done to much damage. I have no desire to reconcile. I could never trust him again.

Reconciliation does not necessarily mean remarriage between divorced partners, although it can certainly lead to that. Author Jim Talley writes, "The primary goal of reconciliation . . . is to enable those of you who are angry, bitter, and hostile to be friendly again and bring back harmony, whether you are already separated, divorced, or remarried."[4]

Instead of just longing for the ways things used to be, it may be possible to better understand each other and cope with potential areas of conflict. But first, the anger has to be defused.

Dr. Talley continues, "I say that reconciliation has been accomplished when both of you can carry on normal human communication. This is a goal to achieve at whatever your legal, moral, or emotional level. Your stomach does not knot up, your blood pressure does not rise anymore, and your voice does not rise in verbal communication."[5]

Once simple communication is restored, you can begin to see your mate as the person he or she really is—and recall why you married in the first place. Remembering why you grew to love your spouse before marriage can provide the incentive for reestablishing friendship—and friendship is imperative in any marriage or reconciliation.

Wait! Before you throw this book into the paper shredder, hear me say that I know reconciliation is not for everyone. My friend, Ann, said, "I don't want to be David's friend. I'm repulsed by his lifestyle and choices."

It was painful and tormenting for Ann to consider whether her marriage could be reconciled. In order to get out of that place of beating herself up, she decided that the real question she had to ask herself was, "Did I do all I could to get counseling from a qualified, respected individual, and am I confident that my choices honored God and myself?

"When I had to pick up my life and make decisions that provided for the well-being of my children and myself, the 'aha' of my experience was realizing I can only be responsible for my choices, not anyone else's."

Some of you share Ann's story, but for others of you who are longing to blow life into the tiny flame still flickering behind your pride or your pain, there may be a reconciliation. There was for me, but it took a lot of self-examination and it took God.

You see, I was an overachiever, a success-oriented, ambitious young woman. I strove for perfection in everything, including my marriage. I filled the cookie jar, made homemade bread, kept our house spotless, and sewed for my whole family. I thought achieving these goals would bring me the attention and approval I wanted from others . . . but especially from my husband.

When it didn't happen, I finally cried out, "If you think I'm going to spend the rest of my life like this, you're crazy!" And my husband and I separated.

In the months that followed I became intimately involved with a stranger named Perceived Failure, and he introduced me to his pal, Deep Depression. My drive to be "supermom" and "superwife" caved into the empty hole in my life.

During this time, I begrudgingly accepted an invitation to go to church with my youngest daughter and her boyfriend. I wasn't in the sanctuary more than a few minutes before I began to suspect that the biggest separation in my life wasn't from my husband; it was from God. As I walked out I asked myself over and over, "What is missing in my life? Could it really be God?"

I quietly slipped into a church the next Sunday. I listened as the Scripture read seemed to pertain to me: "You have been saved through faith, . . . it is a gift from God . . . you can't earn it." Those words from Ephesians 2:8–9 haunted me until, at home, I reread and paraphrased those verses to apply to myself: "For it is because God wants you, Barbara, and you don't even have to work for it; you don't have to bake chocolate-chip cookies or cook a pot roast to earn it, Barbara; you can't earn your way into God's love."

That's when I made the profound discovery that I didn't need to achieve to earn my husband's love either.

Not long after that, I asked both God and my ex-husband to forgive me, and a shaky reconciliation began. In the months that followed I discovered that relating to God enabled me to be a friend again to my husband. It also helped me to come to grips with my drive for perfection.

It was fortunate that neither of us had remarried, and our love could be rekindled. The Justice of the Peace smiled broadly as he read the marriage vows. "My favorite ceremony," he told us, "is for two people who already have the same last name."[6]

———— ❧ ————

Some people continually change jobs,
mates, and friends, but they never
think of changing themselves.
Barbara Johnson[7]

———— ❧ ————

How do you feel about reconciliation? Try to write out your thoughts or desires about reestablishing harmony and friendship with your ex-spouse.

Its not possible. (I shouldn't
say its not possible, with God

76

all things are possible.) But the life style Don is living now makes it impossible for reconcilliation. Beside he is planning on marrying Amy. He's lived with her for almost a year.

Another thing that makes reconcilliation impossible is Don's anger & violence. I can't talk with him without him yelling or calling me names.

A Step of Faith

Reconciliation and peace are often sought but many times not found by the divorced because they look for someone else to change, someone else to humble themselves or give them what they think they want and deserve. Reconciliation and peace must begin with a relationship with Jesus Christ. The one thing worse than living with a mate in disharmony is living with God in disobedience. If you haven't taken that step of faith to ask Jesus to forgive you for your past, to fill the void in your life today and take you to His heaven when you die, I invite you to do that right now before we go further. You see, this act will be the most important step you take toward surviving this difficult time, toward knowing how to move on and reinvest in the rest of your life. You may never reconcile with your ex-spouse, but unless you reconcile with the Father in heaven, you will continue to live with an empty hole in your life.

It is as simple as this prayer:

> *Jesus, the Bible says You died on a cross to pay the penalty for my sins and then lived again after three days. I believe that. I believe that You are the Son of God, and I want You to come into my life, forgive my sins, and give me the desire to live a life pleasing to You. From now on, I will look to You for love, forgiveness, and guidance.*
>
> *Thank you for Your gift of eternal life and for Your Holy Spirit who has now come to live in me to show me how to walk with You for the rest of my life.*
>
> *Amen.*

If you prayed that prayer, write the date here:

_____

I hope you'll tell someone who will rejoice with you. Who will you share this good news with?

_____

_____

_____

The best time of your life may be yet to follow because you took this step of faith. Don't depend on feelings or emotions. Your life will not be without loss or pain or problems, but now you'll have a new source of strength to get you through them.

The good news is that it is never too late to get your life straightened out, to start over, and do what is right.

The story of Job in the Bible is a story of loss and heartbreak. Through no fault of his own, Job lost his wealth, children, and health, and was the laughingstock of his friends. Yet when it seemed nothing was left, Job still had God and that was enough to get him through his pain and help him to start over. In the end "Job did not get back the same children or the same possessions or the same health as he had before . . . what he did get back was a deepened and enlarged capacity for life."[8]

And that, my friend, is my wish and my prayer for you.

Some things I'm thinking, feeling, wishing, hoping, doing:

Date: 3-3-04 - Don is re-married. He got married to Amy on Feb. 20th. I knew it was coming. I'm not sure how I feel. A part of me is happy or glad that they are married. It takes some of the pressure off of me, I think. I don't ever have to take him back if he wants to come back.

Creatively Speaking

— ❧ —

Where there is beauty apparent,
we are to enjoy it;
Where there is beauty hidden,
we are to unveil it;
Where there is beauty defaced,
we are to restore it;
Where there is no beauty at all,
we are to create it.

Robert McAfee Brown

— ❧ —

Creatively Speaking

During a time of intense pain, many people find themselves being surprised by their creativity. Poetry, music, and painting are all outlets for the deepest stirring of the soul. When we give that stirring permission to create, art blooms on the canvas. Fantasy and feeling is set to music. Even journaling takes on the thrill of conceiving a great novel. Each begins with an extension of who we are at that present moment.

For centuries men and women have found poetry to be food for the soul. Poetry whispers healing words to mend a broken relationship and sings a melody to lull a baby to sleep. Poetry with deep feeling and emotion is often birthed by loss.

Father's Day came shortly after my husband and I separated. I wrote this poem for my daughters:

My daughters,
I have loved you since the day you first saw light;
Woven in me, my flesh and blood,
you are an awesome sight.
Please don't weep as I confess
how my marriage has grown cold
like a novel full of heartbreak,
like the moon without the gold.

My dreams are gone,
I have no hope; no solution comes to sight,
I'm weary of the tears and stress
that plague me day and night.
He's moving out, away from home,

running from the pain he feels,
My heart is truly broken;
my wounds need time to heal.

Don't neglect this man who is your dad
on this his special day,
He also hurts and needs your love
to help show him the way
to cope with loss of home and bed
and the future he had planned;
So hurry on, he waits for you with
warmth and outstretched hand.

I remember how sad I felt when the words poured forth into my poem. It brought me in touch with reality. I stood face to face with the poor example I was setting for my daughters whom I'd taught that marriage was forever sacred. There had never been a divorce in my family. Oh, why did I have to be the first?

Sometimes I would dream poetry at night and awaken off and on to write words on a pad by my bed only to be amazed the next morning. No, it wasn't great poetry, but it was healing poetry, for it helped me to bring my pain to the surface. The writing helped me to know that somewhere, deep inside, I was still alive. That restless creativity I had been suppressing for years was breaking through the frozen crust, like a crocus in a snowbank. It helped me to know that my own spring was coming!

For people who have never written poetry, I suggest choosing a nursery rhyme such as "Mary Had a Little Lamb" and listening for the rhythmic beat.

Barbara had an aching heart
Where divorce left a gaping hole.
And everywhere that Barbara went,
The tears were sure to roll.

Now, it's your turn to pick a nursery rhyme and be creative. Write your poem, and then give it a name. Have some fun; try to set your creativity (and your sense of humor) free to soar to new heights. Your poem doesn't have to rhyme; write it any way you wish.

My poem:

_____

_____

_____

_____

_____

_____

_____

_____

Maybe you'd like to set your poem to music. Music is a form of art that also sometimes springs forth from the deep wells of a troubled soul. Has there been a special song that has comforted or lifted your spirits?

'Somebody's Praying Me Thru'

— ❧ —

Next to theology I give to music
the highest place and honor.
Music is the art of the prophets,
the only art that can calm the
agitations of the soul;
it is one of the most magnificent
and delightful presents God has given us.
Martin Luther[1]

— ❧ —

85

Draw a sketch of how you are feeling right now. (Stick figures and childlike artwork will be fine.)

How does the drawing make you feel?

Tired

—— ❧ ——

If your life is windy these days—
winds of change, winds of adversity,
or maybe the constant winds of demands
and expectations that leave you feeling,
well . . . windblown—take heart.
As my mother used to say,
"The roots grow deep when
the winds are strong."
Charles Swindoll[2]

—— ❧ ——

Gifts to Consider

Here are some gifts to give yourself while walking against the winds of divorce:

- ❧ *Time:* Time to be alone and time with people who are willing to listen when you want to talk. Time to pray, time to cry, and time to remember.

- ❧ *Rest:* Extra sleep, unhurried hot baths, naps.

- ❧ *Hope:* Being with others who have "survived" the ordeal of divorce may offer you proof that you can heal.

- ❧ *Goals:* Make a list of goals for today and another one for this week. Unless necessary, don't plan far ahead right now.

- ❧ *Goodness:* Take in a movie, eat a hot-fudge sundae with a friend, sit in a hot tub, or have a massage.

- ❧ *Permission to backslide:* Old feelings of sadness, despair, or anger may return. This is normal and should not be considered failure. Accept it as a "bad day" and remember, "This, too, will pass."

- ❧ *A close friend of the same sex:* It is important that you not attempt to handle your divorce alone. At some time you need to share your responses to what has happened to you with a good friend or someone who can listen objectively. If you become concerned about your progress over a period of nine to twelve months, don't hesitate to get some professional counseling.

Are you feeling change as you journal your feelings and emotions? How?

Date: 3/9/04 • I feel less depressed

I feel more optimistic about

our future. (The Kids & mine). I am

feeling sorry for Don. I don't

~~I wish I could feel~~ . . .

~~Date:~~ have as much hatred towards

him or bitterness. I feel like

Kelsey is doing better because

she is having daily devotions.

I worry about Blake. I'm not sure

how he's handling all this. He doesn't

talk much. He did tell me he doesn't

want to visit his Dad anymore.

I still worry about the kids' safety

when they are with Don. I put this

in Gods hands & ask for wisdom.

His Part, Our Part

I believe the Lord often asks us to do our part before He will do His part. The story of the blind man in John 9:1–11 is a good example of that. The man had been blind since birth and longed to see as others could. When the disciples questioned his blindness, Jesus did a strange thing. He spit in the dirt, making a paste of mud with His saliva. After applying the mud to the eyes of the blind man, Jesus instructed him to go to the pool of Siloam and wash the mud off. When the man did his part, Jesus completed the miracle, and the man received his sight.

At those times when we question our own blindness to why our prayers aren't being answered, we must remember that there may be something Jesus will require of us before our healing can be completed. It may be to admit our part in destroying the marriage. It may be going to our ex-spouse to ask for forgiveness for not keeping the marriage vows.

When unforgiveness holds us in bondage, we can pray and pray, but until we are willing to accept the freedom that Christ can give, we will just stay stuck in the bondage of unforgiveness. We have been blinded by the grief and confusion of our divorce, making it difficult to move on. *You are the only one who can set yourself free.*

Are you unwilling to forgive that person who has hurt you? That's bondage.

Are you worried about what people will think if you admit your own guilt? That, too, is bondage. Stop right now and ask God to reveal all the tentacles of anger, self-pity, and pain that hold you and keep you from complete forgiveness of both yourself and the other people involved. You might want to pray a prayer similar to this:

Dear God, You know my heart better than I do. Please show me any unfinished business that is blocking my healing. I want to put this pain and unforgiveness behind me. Help me not to be so concerned with what others will think of me, but to concentrate on Your plans and designs for my future. Oh, God, forgive me for those times when I chose to stay emotionally frozen in my grief, looking inward instead of keeping my eyes on You.

Thank You for forgiving me and for teaching me to forgive others.

Amen.

Be quiet and allow Him to speak to you. Take your time. As thoughts and decisions come into your mind, make notes so you won't forget them.

Kelsey - Honduras

Dewey & Koko - ?

Dad & Mom - ?

Darla - ?

Magic Moments

At some point, we must realize that we are responsible for our own happiness. We can accept or reject the happiness found in the little things: the tantalizing smell of baking bread, watching a robin splash in the birdbath, or a fireworks display of colored diamonds in the night sky. Those happy, magic moments when an old friend appears at the front door or God says yes to a prayer can renew your energy and improve your disposition.

When magic moments surprise you like an unexpected hug, do you seize it with delight or reject it like an unwelcome suitor?

Seize it

Remember some of your magic moments and how you reacted to them. Record them.

Job interview- Excitement

Kelsey's Academic Letter- Excitement

I surround myself with beauty when I'm in an ugly mood. Beauty creates energy and lifts the spirits. I go out and pick or buy some flowers. Sometimes I walk and let my mind dwell only on the lovely things around me. I try to celebrate each moment as if it were my last day on earth.

How would you celebrate your last day on earth?

With my children Praising God!

We do ourselves a disservice to believe we must have someone to do things with. Aloneness gives us space to grow, time to listen for God's voice, and permission to allow for adjustments in our faith. Aloneness gives us time to evaluate our goals and dreams, to eliminate imperfections that hinder His purpose for us, to try our wings doing new things. Write about your aloneness.

> When the kids are in Iowa, I
> spend alone time shopping or
> scrapbooking. I also spend
> alone time at night after the
> kids are in bed working on this
> book.

Sometimes when I am feeling alone and lonely, I remember reading this:

At first glance, saying God is with you when you're lonely may seem a little impractical when what you really want is a warm body next to yours. But if there isn't a warm body next to yours, you'd better get acquainted with whatever is in second place. And through the experience you might just discover that second place is better than first. God never lets you down. God is always with you. God loves you—no matter what. God wants to bring you only what is best for you. God's best gifts bring you joy. God's shoulder is always ready for you to cry on. Now wherever could you find a better friend than that? Commit your loneliness to God and ask Him to remove it or use it for His glory.[3]

When I do that, contentment creeps in to fill days and nights and, finally, weekends. I have learned that personal contentment is more important than marital companionship. Marriage is not happiness. Happiness is being in the center of God's will.

God calls us to pursue that which He has made available for our happiness. To pursue light in each dark day. To pursue value in a time when it often seems nobody needs us. To pursue our dreams and to delight in God's plan. Psalm 1:2–3 in The Living Bible says, "But they delight in doing everything God wants them to, and day and night are always meditating on his laws and thinking about ways to follow him more closely. They are like trees along a riverbank bearing luscious fruit each season without fail. Their leaves shall never wither, and all they do shall prosper."

Where are you spiritually? Are you a person God can use?

I've always been involved with

small groups or serving God in

Sunday School, AwANA, childrens Church. But I haven't been since the Divorce. I don't feel I can concentrate But I'm getting closer to it.

Read this prayer aloud:

Heavenly Father, sometimes I set the alarm on the timepiece of my loneliness and disappointments. Its jangle drowns out the peace in my soul. It signals how I am hungry in my heart and out of touch with the power. Again and again, God, You awaken me to find that every problem I have is addressed in the Bible. Please autograph it for me with the signature of your unfailing guidance— then hand me Your pen to continue journaling in the next chapter of this book.

Amen.

— ❧ —

You must begin now. There's an old adage that says, "On the plains of hesitation bleach the bones of countless thousands who on the threshold of success sat down to wait and while waiting—wasted and died."

Source unknown

— ❧ —

Some things I'm thinking, feeling, wishing, hoping, doing:

Date: 3-11-04   Kelsey and I are still experiencing ups + downs. Which seem so extreme. Kelsey was so excited about several things; her academic award, getting her letter jacket, Going on a missions trip to Honduras. But then, her Dad comes to her Awards ceremony and cries. He then makes her feel guilty for not including him more. Then she decides not to go out for track because she doesn't want to compete with Dana. So she is really down again. When does this get easier?

Holidays and Special Days

— ✠ —

There is a time for everything, and a season
for every activity under heaven.

Ecclesiastes 3:1

— ✠ —

Holidays and Special Days

Have you any leftover feelings from the last session on creativity? Any new discoveries? Any praises?

_____

_____

Divorce is never smooth and easy. It has ragged edges. As long as you live, you will come face to face with some of those ragged edges. Calling upon God for renewed strength and an adventurer's heart will help. Even a good sense of humor can be a catalyst to the day you'll be able to thank Him for your new experiences and the resulting growth.

Holidays and special days can be unsettling experiences for years after your divorce. Emotions may be more intense as those once-meaningful days approach; however, these are not setbacks. They are just the stumbling blocks in the dark tunnel of sorrow. Knowing they are there can help you to turn them into stepping-stones.

— ✂ —

The Stepping-Stone Prayer
I do not ask to walk smooth paths
Nor bear an easy load.
I pray for strength and fortitude
To climb the rock-strewn road.
Give me such courage I can scale
The hardest peaks alone,
And transform every stumbling block
Into a stepping-stone.
Gail Brook Burket[1]

— ✂ —

Think about a specific day other than what we call "the holiday season" that was special before the separation. For one journaler it was the opening of the summer Olympics. It was a bittersweet day: the excitement and wonderment of the beginning of this remarkable worldwide sports event always competing with the remembrance of twenty years before when her fiancé gave her an engagement ring at McDonald's during the summer Olympics. Was there a special day, one that is perhaps bittersweet for you too?

Christmas

How can you drop the bitter and hang on only to the sweet? This is the way Joyce Lee did it for the first Father's Day after her divorce, which she then wrote about in her journal:

> Today is Father's Day. I'm sorry, Lord, I could not bear to go to church to hear a sermon on fathers, but I was so blessed to go out in your National Forest and take in all of your creation. Your sanctuary was roofed by a blue sky, the walls were fine pine forests, your still waters were the Deschutes River and your celestial choir by the songs of many birds. How I love being your daughter.[2]

Think about how you will deal with the approaching special days.

Wedding anniversary: My plan *I spent it as a normal day.*

Birthdays (his, hers, the children's): My plans

I have to share birthday w/ son. Which I don't think is fair since he's the one that left.

Valentine's Day: ~~My plan~~ *Will always be hard. This is the day Don told the kids.*

Easter: My plan *The kids will be w/ Don. I'm not sure what I'll do.*

Sundays (Sunday afternoons are often said to be the worst hours of the week for the single person.) What plans could you make for Sundays?

Do things w/ the kids on the weekends I have them

You may find yourself writing more notes and lists as the Thanksgiving and Christmas holidays approach. Dealing with being single again is difficult enough without having to think about the "biggies" that come every year, whether we are ready for them or not. However, most people will admit that anticipating the sadness of the special day is worse than the actual day when it comes.

Make some notes here of some holiday things you want to write about, perhaps at a more convenient time.

Don gets the kids for Christmas this year

When faced with a holiday or other special day, ask God to direct how you spend it or to bring someone to help make it easier. He knows your heart, your pain and loneliness, and your need for emotional strength. Those difficult days will pass. Keep your eyes open for turning points.

Surviving Holidays and Anniversaries

At first, most holidays and anniversaries will be difficult for a single-again person. Those special days will now be filled with both sad and glad memories. The most difficult holiday in the calendar is Christmas. It is the one holiday in the United States that no one can avoid. It is in the stores, streets, music, newspapers, magazines; it is on television, radio, in movie theaters, and seemingly even in the air itself. Even long-standing traditions can be difficult to sort out during those perplexing days.

If the tradition no longer fits or is now uncomfortable, consider changing it. Tradition is made for people, not people for tradition. Perhaps it is time to begin a new tradition based on new circumstances.

Make a list of some traditions you want to hold on to. It might be making that creamy chocolate fudge or pulling taffy, having oyster stew after church on Christmas Eve or going Christmas caroling.

1. _Church_

2. _Buying the kids a Christmas ornament_

3. _Spending time at Grandpa+ma Peters_

4. _____

5. _____

6. _____

Which traditions will you let go?

1._____

2._____

3._____

4._____

5._____

6._____

If you are wishing you could go to sleep on December 15 and wake up on December 26, you share the feelings of many other brokenhearted people. If those feelings are honest, don't berate yourself for them. It is simply how you feel at this time. Another year, another time, you will feel differently. The holidays always come around no matter what else happens in life. Ask God to help your desire to celebrate to return.[3]

Men and women everywhere sigh on
December 26 and say they're glad Christmas
is all over for another year. But it isn't over.
"Unto you is born . . . a Savior."
It's just beginning!
And it will go on forever.

Eugenia Price[4]

Because a divorce saps so much physical and emotional strength, this may be a time to beg off from attending that annual office party or other get-together. Don't push yourself. If you don't want to go or if you are too tired, then stay home, rest, and relax. Are you being pushed to do something that is difficult this year?

Milligan's wanted me to go to their house for X-mas. It was just to hard to go.

How will you deal with it?

Thanking them but not going

Restaurants stay open on most holidays knowing that some people will not want to prepare a large meal and clean up afterward. Consider eating out if you want to have a large meal. A quiet snack alone is also acceptable.

Write about your holiday meal preferences now, and then come back to this book and review it when the actual holiday arrives.

Have your desires changed?

For many people, being in their place of worship during holiday festivities can be painful. The ritual of the services, the music, prayers, and even people at church may seem difficult; however, it is important to attend church if at all possible in order to be a part of the corporate worship. Hopefully, you will sense a shelter from your storm there and can turn your eyes and heart to the One whose birthday we celebrate. Like Bill Butterworth, it may change your life. In his book, *When Life Doesn't Turn Out Like You Planned*, he wrote,

Without question, a real turning point for me in my spiritual journey came the Sunday of the first Christmas I was single again. What had always been the highlight of the year, December 25, was now an awkward occasion of negotiating "who had whom" from "when to when" and how to best handle the minutiae of keeping Christmas special to the kids when inside I was a brokenhearted wreck.

As I walked into the sanctuary that Sunday before Christmas, the room was warmly decorated with wreaths and ribbons and lanterns. The central focus, however, was a life-size manger, placed on the floor in front of the pulpit. Real straw was brimming from the four sides of the manger, and it wonderfully re-created what the Christ-child must have lain in on that cold winter's night.

When Ed stood up to preach that morning, I had already wept quietly several times as we sang a procession of well-known Christmas carols. Each song was pregnant with memories of Christmases past, when everything in the world was so much better.

I wonder what Ed will say this year? I found myself thinking before he began. There are only so many ways you can find meaning in gold, frankincense, and myrrh, for example, and no room at the inn only can go so far in its practical application.

Ed chose to go deeper into Luke's gospel account, later in the life of Christ. He chose as his text a verse from the fourth chapter, when Jesus was actually a grown man. But it was a verse that was especially relevant to the Christmas season. . . . Isaiah had spoken those words centuries before in prophecy of the coming Messiah.

> *The Spirit of the LORD GOD is upon me,*
> *Because the LORD has anointed me*
> *To bring good news to the afflicted;*
> *He has sent me to bind up the brokenhearted,*
> *To proclaim liberty to captives,*
> *And freedom to prisoners.* (Isaiah 61:1 NASB)

When Ed finished reading Isaiah's words, it was as if there was no longer anyone else in the worship service. I felt as if he were speaking directly to me and me alone. He chose to zero in on a key phrase— "He sent me to bind up the brokenhearted."

"Is this year a difficult Christmas for you?" Ed asked. "Are you brokenhearted over a circumstance that has left you in great pain?"

Tears were streaming down my cheeks as I knew that this was a message from God for me. All that moisture dripping down onto my lap was silently answering Ed, "Yes . . . yes . . . I am brokenhearted."

Meanwhile Ed had moved from his position behind the pulpit to a place in front of it. Standing over the manger, he crouched down and said, "If you're here in deep pain, I want you to do something for me. I invite you to leave your burden here in the manger. For remember, Jesus Christ has come to mend that which is torn inside of you. He has come to bind up your broken heart."

I don't remember much of what happened after that, except that in my soul, I gave Christ all the pain my crisis had created. It wasn't the sort of thing that was accompanied by harps, strings, or chills up the spine, but it was an awesomely moving encounter for me. In many ways, it was like nothing I had ever experienced.

Christmas was bearable, thanks to Him who had come to bind up my broken heart. I was so grateful that I had made this discovery at what could have been the most awful time of the year. God was loving me, healing me, and giving me strength. In God's great timing, He was allowing me to experience a spiritual high.[5]

You can never truly enjoy Christmas until you can look up into the Father's face and tell him you have received his Christmas Gift.

John R. Rice[6]

Like Bill, you may have had a holiday experience that was meaningful for you. Write about that. Use additional paper if you need it. Save your story—you may wish to share it another time, perhaps to help others through their difficult holidays.

Christmas was spent with Rhonda & Randy. I had the kids. Rhonda & Randy made it very special. They gave me a pair of diamond earings. I've always wanted a pair.

Especially on gift-giving days, it is not uncommon for people to try to buy their way out of guilt and heartache. It happens with the spouse who does not have custody of the children; it happens with concerned grandparents, as if toys could ever replace having both Mom and Dad present at Christmas.

Adults do it for themselves, too, buying new furniture, clothes, or perhaps taking an extravagant weekend trip. This is a time to watch your spending. Has there been a time you tried to buy your way out of heartbreak?

I did go over board with the kids at Christmas. I was trying to make up for their Dad.

I remember feeling such a sense of aloneness on Valentine's Day because I was no longer anyone's sweetheart. I felt especially lonely and very single when the Valentine's dinner was announced at church; however, I pretended not to care. A week before the dinner, a married couple in the church invited me to attend with them. Before I could object, the man assured me he had two arms, one for his wife and one for me to hold on to as we walked into the dinner.

It was difficult to refuse, so I accepted the invitation. The man brought me a corsage, just like his wife's. He held my chair as I sat down at the table. That wonderful evening reinforced the message that I didn't have to be married to have a good time.

On this page, describe how you would like to spend one of the coming holidays.

Easter - I would like to go to Church with my kids. Sing praises to God with them. Celebrate Christs raising from the dead.

What is keeping you from realizing this desire?

The kids will be with Don for Easter.

I read this testimonial in the "Dear Abby" column in my local newspaper and thought it worth sharing with you:

> Dear Abby:
>
> I have something to say to the millions of families whose lives are affected by divorce.
>
> An unforgiving and bitter person who has not let go of animosities can poison an entire family and ruin the holidays for everyone. I know. I was that person.
>
> I couldn't forgive my husband and his new wife, and my children suffered for it. One day after a particularly harsh outburst, I understood the pained reaction on my children's faces. I prayed for the strength to change my ways so I could stop hurting those I love most in the world.
>
> It has been a long struggle with occasional setbacks, but the rewards have carried me forward. I have not remarried and I am not completely healed, but I have peace in my heart and my children are happy. They are free to enjoy both homes and the holidays with each family. It is a priceless gift to give your children, and yourself.
>
> Free in Vermont[7]

A Safe Haven on Difficult Days

"If instead of finding peace on earth you find your emotions in a war zone"[8] during the coming holiday season, you're not alone. Marianne Hering offers some suggestions:

- ☙ Focus on spiritual essentials. Instead of cluttering your holidays with a frenzy of trivial activities, schedule time for events that will nurture your spirit. Check the newspaper to find out which churches are hosting special musicals or Advent services.

- ☙ Get in touch with friends. Make a commitment to phone at least three friends who are on your Christmas card list. Those conversations could become a catalyst for reminding you of good times or give you that unexpected job lead or new perspective on a personal problem.

- ☙ Let the tears flow. If strong, sad memories of holidays past are overwhelming you, take them seriously and act while the feelings are at the surface. Set aside some private time to reflect on the past. Make an appointment to grieve. According to scientists, crying helps relieve stress and is good for mental health.

- ☙ Bring the gift of compassion. Odds are that others are dealing with a sense of loss as well during holidays. You can give them solace.[9]

Instead of counting losses, count new faces sitting around the table. Fill empty chairs with friends. Many of you have made new friends because of the changes in who you are now.

And some of you honored a commitment to take this journey with a friend and to support each other over the finish line. Good for you!

Today as you read and write and listen to your heart, do you realize you have scaled a mountain? I hope you are pleased with yourself for sticking to your commitment to keep climbing (even if you occasionally skin your shins) until you find a place to unload and come to grips with your divorce.

Use this space to make notes about ways of handling difficult days that this chapter or your friends and family have brought to your attention.

Easter - Go to church w/ Randy Rhonda & the girls.

Christmas - I'm not sure.

February - The hardest month of the year. Go to Hawaii!

For six weeks or more you have been journaling about the pain of the loss of your marriage. By now you must suspect that there is life after a divorce. There is light at the end of the tunnel, and it's not a train speeding toward you. As your eyes begin to focus, you can start setting goals, you can solo, and you can recover. Are you ready? _Yes!!_

You will know you're beginning to recover when:

- ❧ taking care of yourself is not only okay, but it feels good

- ❧ the future is not so frightening

- ❧ you can handle "special days and holidays" without falling apart

- ❧ you want to reach out to others whose hearts have been broken

- ❧ your emotional roller coaster is slowing down

- ❧ you forget and forgive the injustices that once hurt so deeply

A Christmas Wish from Me to You

In the words of Bishop Remington:

> I am wishing for you this day a happy Christmas. I would send you those gifts which are beyond price, outlast time, and bridge all space. I wish you all laughter and pure joy, a merry heart and a clear conscience, and love which thinks no evil, is not easily provoked, and seeks not its own; the fragrance of flowers, the sweet associations of holly and mistletoe and fir, the memory of deep woods, of peaceful hills, and of mantling snow, which guards the sleep of all God's creatures. I wish that the spirit of Christmastide may draw you into companionship with him who giveth all.
>
> Come, let us adore him.[10]

Some things I'm thinking, feeling, wishing, hoping, doing:

Date: 3-16-04 I'm wanting to move on with my life. I want to get a great job. One with benefits, with decent pay, close to home! (I applied for a job at Rural Community Insurance Companies.) It is the perfect job. I have faith that I will get this job. God provided the interview. He will provide the job!

Moving On!

— ❧ —

*The waste of life lies
in the love we have not given,
the powers we have not used,
the selfish prudence which will
risk nothing and which,
shirking pain, misses
happiness as well.*

Author unknown

— ❧ —

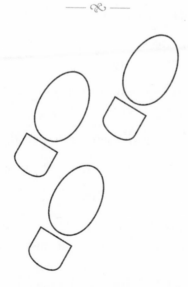

New Beginnings

Everyone was seated for session 7 of one of my journaling groups. I'd baked a fancy dessert and tied balloons to the chairs. As I lit a candle in preparation to open this final meeting, I noticed one of the women distributing plastic sandwich bags full of an assortment of things to each person. This distraction was not in my plans; however, it will be from now on.

She called it a "Care Kit." It contained a list that described the bag's contents:

- A *paper clip*—to help keep things together when they seem to be slipping out of control.

- A *rubber band*—to remind you that there is always someone to offer a hug when you need it.

- A *tissue*—to wipe away a tear—your own or someone else's.

- A *candy kiss*—to say "I Love You" in a very special way.

- An *eraser*—to erase any mistake or misunderstanding that is bothering you.

- A *note card*—to send a greeting to a friend or relative who is lonely.

- A *recipe*—to make something special for someone.

- A *poem*—to share the beauty of words.

- A *Scripture verse*—to share God's Word.

- An *adhesive bandage*—to remind you of healing—perhaps of hurt feelings, your own or someone else's.

I examined each treasure from the plastic bag, pondering on the appropriateness of each piece. A simple, plastic sandwich bag, yet it bulged with tidbits of healing, compassion, forgiveness, hope, love, and generosity. At first I thought the only thing missing was a way to begin treasuring their new lives. But then I found it was there in the poem she had included in the bag:

Happiness is like a crystal,
Beautiful and clear,
Broken in a thousand pieces
And scattered far and near.
Into your life some pieces
Are surely chanced to fall;
Treasure each most dearly
For you'll never find them all.[1]

Into each of your lives, some treasure has fallen, none alike. Can you take what you have been given and offer it up to a perfect God who loves and uses imperfect people? When we can do that, we don't get so centered in our own desires but we discover God's treasures for us at this point in our lives.

As I was considering how to suggest ways for you to do that, my pastor preached a sermon about a man named Elijah in 1 Kings 19. Elijah was depressed. He moaned, "It is enough. Take my life." Elijah's life hadn't turned out the way he planned.

Pastor Syd said Elijah's problem was "spiritual depression." *It happens when we begin to replay the old grievances.* We need to be reminded that *whatever shapes our thinking shapes our life.*

When we (as Elijah did) get spiritually depressed, we become targets for satanic assault. We become careless and fail to check our armor. Sometimes we go into isolation or a self-imposed exile, thereby losing our support system.

God asked Elijah, "What are you doing there?" I believe He asks the same question of us. Elijah was an imperfect person, *like us*, and God went to great lengths to bring him out of his spiritual depression and provide what he needed. He did not abandon Elijah nor will He abandon us, but we must refuse to play those negative tapes from our past that drown out His voice. Consider these ways to respond to any reoccurring despair and disappointment.

1. Prayer must take its place in every day. Billy Graham wrote, "I have never met a person who spent time in daily prayer and in the study of God's Word . . . who was ever discouraged for very long."[2] "In the morning, prayer is the key that opens to us the treasures of God's mercies and blessings; in the evening, it is the key that shuts us up under His protection and safeguard."[3] How are you doing with this one?

Good I read my bible every morning & pray. I am concerned about making time for this once I work.

2. It is important for single people to seek out a fellow believer (of the same sex) to lean on and to support. "Two are better than one" does not say the two need to be married. "Two are better than one" so that one may hold the other up during times of crisis and weakness. In Ecclesiastes 4:9–10, 12 we're told, "Two are better than one. . . . If one falls down, his friend can help him up. But pity the man who falls and has no one to help him up! . . . Though one may be overpowered, two can defend themselves. A cord of three strands is not quickly broken."

You, a friend, and Jesus: a cord of three strands. How does this relate to you right now?

I have a great support system.
Randy & Rhonda — Jane, Kim, Mary,

3. *We must reenter the game.* God permits in our lives only those negative events that He plans to use to make us grow. If the trials were just "cured" or "taken away," we would not be any more mature even though we were no longer in pain. Without change, we would not be equipped to reenter the game of life. List some ways you have matured since your marriage vows were severed.

I feel closer to God
I'm stronger — I don't need to
depend on someone.

— ❧ —

And the God of all grace who called you to
his eternal glory in Christ, after you have
suffered a little while, will himself restore you
and make you strong, firm and steadfast.
1 Peter 5:10

— ❧ —

Inhale deeply. In every breath of life there lies a purpose for you alone—exciting and exhilarating enough to give you momentum to pursue dreams with a passion and to reinvest in goals that have lain dormant.

"For I know the plans I have for you," declares the LORD, "plans to prosper you and not to harm you, plans to give you hope and a future. Then you will call upon me and come and pray to me, and I will listen to you. You will seek me and find me when you seek me with all your heart."

Jeremiah 29:11–13

This last session is for dreamers—people who set goals, wish on stars, and look for rainbows. In choosing to move on, you have chosen to step out of the darkness, to turn the corner and shout for all the world to hear, "I am a survivor!"

Think about and note one particular time when you realized you were a survivor!

When I made it thru the one year anniversary of the Divorce. Seeing how far Ive come.

Setting Goals

Make two lists—one of short-term goals you'd like to reach in the next one to three months, and the other of long-term goals set for the next one to three years.

Example:

Short-term goals:

1. Join an athletic club and work out.
2. Make a budget and balance the checkbook.
3. Invite a friend to supper at your home.
4. Take the kids overnight to the beach.
5. Wallpaper a room or buy some drapes.
6. Sing in the choir or try out for a drama in your church.

List your short-term goals.

exercise 3x week   *Make time for friends*

get a job _____

join a small group _____

Start paying off bills _____

What do you think of when you hear about long-term goals? Some examples are:

1. Purchase a home.
2. Take a long-dreamed-of vacation.

3. A job promotion or own your own business.

4. Get married again.

5. Go to college.

Make your own list.

Advance at job   start dating
Buy a new vehicle   possibly marriage
Pay off bills   go to Hawaii
Buy a house or town house

—— ❧ ——

Some people fail to reach their full potential of
a rewarding harvest in life because they have
not turned their dreams into specific goals and
plans of action for reaching those goals.

Denis Waitley[4]

—— ❧ ——

Describe how or when you can begin to work on some of your goals.

The first step is to get this
job I applied for. The rest
will follow

122

Is something keeping you from setting yourself free to pursue the rest of your life without having to look back? Can you name it? ___*Nothing*___

If you are still holding on to anger, that means you are still attached to the person who offended you. How can you let go of any remaining anger, unresolved pain and hurt, depression and grief? You must *choose!* No one can choose for you. No one can solo for you. There are no prizes for spectators, only for participants.

When you discover the treasures that await you outside of marriage, you have made peace with your divorce. It will only be then that you are free to live life to its fullest measure. *Other people will find pleasure in your company only if you have learned to find pleasure in yourself.*

I will seek the Lord to renew my strength.
I will soar on wings like eagles.
I will run but not be weary; walk and not grow faint.
I will solo and not be lonely.
Isaiah 40:31 (Author's paraphrase)

There is value in soloing. In an airplane, you must first know the controls and who controls them. In life after divorce, the same principle applies.

No matter what you do for the first time, it's important that you reach out to take the hand of the One who said He would never leave you. He'll walk beside you, and His strength and stamina will flow through your veins. And when you tire, He'll carry you. Let Him!

Celebrate!

After the icy winds of divorce have ceased to blow through the heart, there comes a new season and with it a "Moving On Celebration." Begin now. How will you celebrate this week?

- Invite a friend to a ball game.

- Buy some new sheets.

- Share a banana split with someone.

- Sit in a hot tub.

- Cook dinner in a wok.

Add your own celebration ideas.

- *Go out to lunch*
- *Buy new jeans*
-
-

The weekend before I finished this final chapter I visited the site of the volcanic eruption at Mount St. Helens in the state of Washington. I remember the headline news on May 18, 1980, when the elegantly forested landscape surrounding the mountain was transformed into an inferno. From my home in Oregon, I watched the television coverage of a 9,677-foot summit reduced by 1,300 feet in a matter of only moments. During the 9-hour eruption, 500-million cubic yards of molten rock were blasted from the mountain, creating an ash cloud that rose 12 miles into the atmosphere. The elevation of Spirit Lake was raised 200 feet as the result of materials from the mountain being deposited into it. Fifty-seven people were killed. Some two hundred more fled in fear to safety, their lives forever changed.

As I stood looking at magnificent Mount St. Helens, my thoughts strayed to those of you who would someday read this book. You fit into the postcard I'd just purchased: the eruption of that marriage "made in heaven," the blast of harsh words, the homes splintered and divided up, the landslide of broken lives forever changed. My heart felt heavy.

Then, as I participated in the tourist activities at each of the four visitor's centers on the way up to the base of the mountain, I began to catch glimpses of hope. The forest rangers spoke of the healing of the land, the transformation, the slow process of recovery that has steadily taken place until signs of the tranquil beauty of the future can already be seen. The volcano, first known as an ugly witch, is well on its way to becoming a beautiful maiden.

Again, I thought of you.

Within weeks of the eruption, despite early concerns about whether the forest environment would, or even could, recover, fireweed, thistle, and blackberry began to reappear. Small burrowing animals, such as mice and gophers, survived the surface blast. Within a year, a carpet of fireweed covered the thin ash layers near Ryan Lake, and the returning plants have attracted insects and birds. Now, on the pumice plains, fir trees have found footholds. The Roosevelt elk and the golden-mantled ground squirrel have returned home.

The miracles and mysteries I beheld by the time I reached the last visitor's center and stared into the crater of the mountain told me that you, too, would survive. Like the mountain, you have survived the blast. You can weather and recover from your divorce; you will bloom again. And I applaud you!

In closing this final chapter, I share the words my friend wrote as she approached the first page of her second journal on New Year's Day.

This is the second year I will be keeping a journal. The first was last year when my world was shaken apart by David's drive to get a divorce. But through all of that, my journaling provided great insight to the presence of the Lord, for through the very worst [times] of my life, I have seen His faithfulness, love and provision. I journal to know Him more fully. It has become very evident to me that keeping a journal allows me to give God the glory for all He's done for me on a daily basis. I worship an awesome God who I know will stay with me—in good times and bad.[5]

As you complete this journal, you have seen firsthand how the challenges of divorce can be met not only with acceptance of what has happened but with dignity and assurance that God created only one you and you are precious in His sight. "The most powerful statement we can make to a watching world is that our God is worthy of our affection and allegiance—even through the rough times."[6]

It has been a privilege to offer this unique resource and support tool for the divorced, believing it is possible to put the past behind and celebrate those good qualities with which God has blessed you (and me) as a unique individual.

To an awesome God, I offer praise and honor and gratitude for leading the way through that passage called divorce.

Hugs!

Barbara Baumgardner

Epilogue

The last page of this book does not end your journey. Chances are you will find times when expressing your deepest feelings can be done best on paper.

I want to challenge you to continue journaling in another book, on another day, in a way that brings emotional release that is both restful and satisfying. Don't make any "I will make an entry every day or else" rules. Write when you feel like it or when you have something to record that you don't want to forget. It is okay to have days when you forget to write. Never forget that putting your thoughts and emotions on paper is a good way of getting things out and setting them in order.

The years, months, and hours that remain in your life are yours to spend any way you choose. Do not waste them, but pursue the rest of your life without self-pity or resentment. This is the time to concentrate on your own life, not on the mate you are no longer joined to. When you discover purpose in living, your hopes and dreams will be filled with joy, peace, and contentment.

Above all else, I encourage you to walk with God. "God's laws and principles are good. They are intended to keep us out of harm's way and direct us in ways that ultimately bless and prosper our lives."[1]

Poet Carl Sandburg said, "Life is like an onion; you peel it off one layer at a time, and sometimes you weep."[2]

Weeping is often necessary to get to the core of our life.

Periods of our life make us weep—like that awful day we had to face the reality of divorce. Under the layers of tears, anguish, heartache, and doubts, it was hard to imagine finding a core that would be sweet and desirable.

My prayer for you is that during the next months and years, you will allow Jesus Christ to tap into each layer of your life to continue the healing of the grief and pain that brought you to this book. I pray that you will allow Him to touch you with the joy that comes in the morning like sunshine after the rain.

For I am convinced that neither death
nor life, neither angels nor demons,
neither the present nor the future,
nor any powers, neither height nor depth,
nor anything else in all creation,
will be able to separate us from the love of
God that is in Christ Jesus our Lord.

Romans 8:38–39

Final notes about some things I'm thinking, feeling, wishing, hoping, doing:

Date: 3-17-04 - I find it so very comforting to come to the end of this journaling book the very day that I find out I got the job I wanted. God is so awesome! I'm starting a new journey in my life as I close an old one. I never wanted this Divorce to happen but happen it Did. It has brought me closer to God. I've learned to have faith & trust in him to provide. God you are all I need. Thank you! Thank you!

CONGRATULATIONS!

This certifies that

_____

has successfully completed A *Passage through Divorce* program.

Group Leader: _____

Date: _____

— ❧ —

*May the God of hope fill you with all joy
and peace as you trust in him,
so that you may overflow with hope
by the power of the Holy Spirit.*
                                        Romans 15:13

— ❧ —

Leader's Guide

❧

Do not fear, for I am with you,
do not be afraid, for I am your God;
I will strengthen you, I will help you,
I will uphold you with my
victorious right hand.

Isaiah 41:10 NRSV

❧

Introduction

Leading a divorce recovery journaling group can be an enjoyable and rewarding experience. It will also stretch and may intimidate you—especially if you've never done it before.

Some experience in grief, journaling, and divorce will help you be an effective group leader. Other qualifications include a compassionate heart, a love for reading and writing, and a sincere desire to help hurting people.

Stability in your own emotions is also important in order to cope with the tears, anger, and feelings of rejection and loneliness that surface in a group of single-again people. If you have been divorced or very close to a divorce situation, your own circumstances may help to equip you as a leader. Without most of these characteristics, you may find that the role of a divorce-recovery facilitator is simply not your niche.

It is vital to remember that the men and women who attend any support or recovery group are extremely vulnerable. Caution should be exercised when offering advice, especially based on your own experiences. The people attending your group are looking to you for hope, not pat answers.

There is a significant increase in the rate of suicide among those who are mourning the loss of their marriage. Watch for signs of unresolved conflict and ongoing depression. Don't hesitate to seek out professional help when the need arises, especially when the sorrowing person continually writes or talks about having no reason or desire to live.

Got butterflies? Great! You are about to journey down an intriguing pathway into a world laced with pain and frustration, yet in spite of all the rocky obstacles, you'll see miracles happen. As you touch the lives of others with this program of support and education, you will also be touched by their lives, their love, kindness, and respect, and their friendship.

Remember, it is usually the facilitator who learns the most—so step out, lead on, and grow!

My prayer for you:

Lord, I thank You for Your promise that You will never leave us or forsake us. I thank You that You are willing to take the sorrow and emotional pain from the lives of these dear ones who desire healing from the loss of a marriage they once believed would last forever. I ask for that healing for each one who has had the courage to step out in this difficult time to say, "I need help. I need to learn to live as a single person again."

I ask, Lord, that You will take charge of this class, that You will reshape lives and convert struggles into energy, prayer, and courage. Change these lives to see they can have value again. Show them how to look to You to fill their days and nights with peace and joy and healing.

And Lord I ask You to equip this dear person to be a servant facilitator who will listen to Your leading and allow You to be the teacher and healer during these sessions.

We welcome Your presence in this divorce recovery workshop.

In Your precious name,
Amen.

Preparing for a Divorce-Grief Journaling Group

Date and Time

Set a weekly meeting. Early evening from 6:30 to 8:00 P.M. works well. Many divorced people hold down a full-time job, so this is usually a workable time. They have time to have a quick supper, attend the meeting, and still get home at a decent hour. However, those with small children may need to meet on a Saturday morning or late in the evening. Because each group will vary, you'll need to find the time that is comfortable for the most people. An hour and a half gives time for work but not much socializing.

Check local community calendars to be sure there is no holiday or other conflict with your choice of day. Try not to change the meeting time once it is established, because the stress of change may cause people to be confused and forgetful.

Begin and end the meeting on time.

Advertise

Put notices on community bulletin boards and in newsletters, and call churches to tell them of your intent to lead a divorce recovery journaling group. Most churches need help with the divorced in their congregation, especially when the pastor and staff have no personal divorce experience or even available laypeople to come alongside those who are struggling with divorce. An announcement in church bulletins or newsletters may bring someone to your journaling group.

Ask the special events editor of your local newspaper to write a story. List your meeting in community event bulletins and in television and radio public service announcements.

Warning! Don't get too many people in your group. Six is perfect, eight is workable, but more than that doesn't allow enough time for reading and sharing in an hour and a half to two hours.

Another warning! Please don't ever try to combine divorced people with people who are grieving the death of a loved one into one support group. There will be misunderstandings, jealousy, and hurt feelings. Yes, there is grief and mourning in both losses, but too often a recently widowed person will say, "Well, at least she or he is still alive," only to be answered by the divorced person saying, "Well, at least you don't have to see them with the new love in their life."

For those who need help with recovery from a death, please refer them to my previous book, *A Passage through Grief: An Interactive Journal* also published by Broadman & Holman.

Be Prepared

Review the session notes and leader's guide before arriving at the meeting location. A lonely journaler may arrive early, distracting you from what you planned to be your study time. Advance preparation also gives you time to thoughtfully consider what might be the reaction of the journalers to the material you will be presenting. How can you encourage them to take the risk of sharing their innermost feelings with those around them?

Plan for your time to be disrupted by emotion and by those who need to talk. On the other hand, if the group is noncommunicative, you may find time needing to be filled. Consider ways to fill that time with hope. Suggestions are given with each session.

Participants will need to have their own copy of the book *A Passage through Divorce* to read and write in. It works well for group leaders to purchase the required number of copies prior to the first meeting and then ask to be reimbursed for the cost. However, a leader may request that participants purchase their own copy at a bookstore prior to the first meeting. Give your local bookstore at least two weeks' notice so they can have enough copies on hand for your group.

A break is usually not appropriate in the middle of these sessions as it stops the flow of communicating feelings. As participants begin to bond and share, extra time may be needed for socializing after the session ends.

Welcome, Warmth, and Encouragement Are Vital

Remember, journaling is not for everyone and most people will feel intimidated at first. A soft drink, coffee, or tea with a cookie can ease the tension and calm the fears before the first meeting. Simple refreshments should be ready so that valuable class time is not used waiting for people to finish eating.

If someone has had a particularly bad week, mail the person a note of encouragement or telephone them between sessions.

Always be on the lookout for outside sources of help: articles, stories, bookmarks, poems, or greeting cards to share with the group as "extra treats" to be tucked into the back of their journaling workbook.

During the Session

One of the major jobs of a facilitator is to pace the study. Open with a sincere interest in what kind of week they've had, or significant happenings. One woman excitedly reported that for the first time since she'd been alone again, she had all her bills paid. The group rejoiced with her.

Ask questions that draw them into discussion, as this will enable them to be comfortable with reading aloud. A journaler found the courage to write about her angry, rebellious son after being asked how she and the son were doing alone. She was relieved to find it was okay to share this pain.

Note that each session has its own suggested opening in the journaling workbook. Read this aloud. Ask for feedback such as "How did that make you feel?" or "Tell me how you identify with that" or "Has this happened to you?"

Review the list of "ground rules" on pages 142–143 in this leader's section as often as appropriate. It is not fair if one person dominates the time, depriving others of an opportunity to speak. A quick review of rules can be a reminder.

Those attending these journaling sessions may want to hear bits and pieces of your own life in order to know you as a person, not just as their facilitator. The human side of you—your downfalls as well as victories with your own journey through divorce—can be shared briefly. This will help them to know that you truly can relate to their loss.

The group facilitator does not read from his or her own journal. Keep in mind that your job is to help the group members discover ways to keep from "stuffing" their pain. Journaling is one of their tools. They need to focus on their healing, not on you.

Let the workbook help you moderate discussions, draw in quieter members, and pace the study. Encourage people to interact with each other's observations. Volunteer your own reactions only to offer encouragement and hope.

Make notes while participants are reading their journals aloud. Use them as guidelines for discussion such as, "You wrote about the problem of finding a new place to park your boat since you moved from the home. Is that resolved now?" or, "Were you angry at him for blowing his paycheck?" Encourage group participation.

Be alert to particular needs in the group. Sometimes, you may need to abandon even the best-laid plans in order to tend to "emotion emergencies." When other group members reach out to comfort and support a distraught member, a few minutes of the session may be lost, but important bonding and friendships are gained.

Contact with one another outside the meeting can be as valuable as the meeting itself, so after three or four sessions, a luncheon could be scheduled for the entire group. As a leader, you do not need to feel compelled to attend. It is important for the divorced to find support away from you.

Review the list of additional resources and suggested reading at the end of the workbook when you have time to fill. Suggest that the people check out the local library for books or videos on the topic of divorce. If some of the books listed in my suggested reading list on page 161 are not in stock, you'll find most bookstores are willing to order them.

A word of caution if you recommend books to your group: Know the contents of the book. For example, I've encountered several divorce self-help books that suggest lifestyles that do not match with Christian principles as a way to ease the pain.

The following pages will lead you through all of the sessions in this workbook. No group-leading experience is necessary as you follow the leader's guide through each class as outlined.

You will find places to share your own experiences, and you'll learn to leave out what is not appropriate for your unique group.

Bon voyage! Have a wonderful and satisfying journey as you lead some hurting, needy people beside still waters to a peaceful place called hope.

Session 1

Introduce yourself as the facilitator. Pass around a sign-in sheet and name tags. Encourage large, printed names that can be seen across the table. Read or explain the following in your own words:

> For session 1, I will do much of the talking except to have you introduce yourselves so we can begin to know each other. But the next time, it will be your turn, and I won't talk so much.
>
> It has taken a lot of courage for you to come. It is hard to come to a group when you might not know anyone, but even harder when you are dealing with such intimate issues. Today will be the hardest session. When you get ready to come next week, the anxiety you are feeling now won't be as severe because you'll know more of what to expect when you walk into the room.
>
> Please don't let your apprehension get in the way of your participating and benefiting from this group. [If you want to lead the group in some deep breathing or relaxing exercises, now would be the time to do that. You might find it helpful to have an icebreaker activity.]
>
> It is important that you attend regularly. I'm asking you to make a commitment to be here, not only for yourself but for the other group members. However, if you must miss, do that session at home so you can keep up with the rest of the group.

Review these weekly sessions at home. Read them over and over if necessary. You may not understand all the information given, so I encourage you to ask questions during the meetings.

When we finish six or seven weeks from now, we will have examined a lot of divorce recovery helps, as well as the journaling. Hopefully, you will have recognized some significant signs of recovery in yourself.

Beginning today, you are going to make some new friends—some you may have for the rest of your life. This will not be a confrontational group—our approach is one of gentleness and acceptance. We encourage participation because you will benefit more if you are involved. But we recognize that quiet people get a lot out of these groups as well as the more talkative ones.

Reactions to the writing you do will be nonjudgmental. You see, grief is unique to each individual. We all own our *own* feelings; it is not our job to give advice or to criticize one another.

However, if you have any stories, poems, or letters that have helped you in the process of your divorce, please feel free to bring them and, as time permits, share them. I don't have all the answers, so your sharing may benefit us all.

We do have some "Ground Rules." [Note: Read aloud or ask participants to take turns reading from the leader's guide in the back of their own books.]

1. Confidentiality is essential. We may hear or share some personal and private information. To feel safe, we need to know that what we share doesn't go outside this group. We will be trusting others with a piece of our hearts.

2. *It is okay to say "pass."* You are not obligated to talk or share if you feel uncomfortable doing so.

3. *We speak for and about ourselves only.* We are here to deal with our own divorce, not that of another person.

4. *Everyone should have an opportunity to share.* One of the roles of the facilitator is to make sure no one talks too long, so sometimes I become a timekeeper.

If you need to talk about something that you are not comfortable bringing up in the group session, you may call me for an appointment. If I can't help, I may suggest you see a counselor.

5. *We will allow newcomers next week only.* After the second week, the group will be closed. If you must drop out, a telephone call would be considerate to let your fellow members know.

6. *Know that feelings and emotions will surface during our time together.* It is okay to cry. Healing occurs through expressing and sharing our feelings. [Note: A box or two of tissues should be within reach.]

Turn to page 3 and follow along while I read it aloud. It explains the process of journaling your pain. [It also works well to ask each person to read a paragraph aloud here. Watch for boredom as you read to them. Minds are on overload, and they need to participate as much as possible.]

Introduce yourself briefly again. Ask others to share what brought them here, how they heard about this group, and what they hope to get out of it.

Turn to pages 5–6 as you begin and as needed throughout introductions. Use it as a reference for those who have difficulty telling about their loss.

Allow about thirty minutes for a group of six people to share. (Take notes for future reference about their losses or needs.) Call attention to the quote on page 6.

If you have less than fifteen minutes before ending this session, just walk through the rest of the pages in session 1 with the group. Explain how pages 6–9 will help get them started writing something to be read aloud next week. It need not be long, but do encourage them to write something.

Make sure the group knows that the writing examples in the workbook are included with the author's permission as encouragement for those who undertake this journaling program.

If you have men in your group, congratulate them for their willingness to face their divorce head-on, because many men are not able to do that. Read the "Men and Divorce" aloud if time permits, and allow the men in the group to comment.

Use the following two pages to close session 1, or to fill extra time in another session:

Why Divorce-Grief Recovery Is Important

The loss of someone significant from your life brings a lot of pain and change. This can produce bitterness and illness, but support + pain + change produces growth.

Many people "stuff" their pain by trying to keep very busy. Others run away from the pain—some even get remarried to try to avoid it. But the sooner and more intensely you mourn the loss, the sooner you will heal.

As with a death in the family, there is a huge increase in illness of those involved in a divorce. The immune system doesn't function very well when people are impacted by rejection, sorrow, and unwanted change.

Also, there is an increase in vandalism, delinquency, alcohol consumption, illicit relationships, and suicide among both the young and old.

An earlier unresolved loss makes it more difficult to resolve current losses (even the loss of a family pet).

With a support system, these trends are reversed.

When grief is denied, ignored, or buried it waits for us. It will come up at a later time, and that may be an even more difficult time to deal with it.

What Factors Make It Difficult for People to Grieve a Divorce?

- ❧ The lack of support systems due to the mobility and uprootedness of American families.

- ❧ People who expect the divorced to "Hurry up and get over it" in two or three weeks.

⮞ No one brings a casserole or shows sympathy for the loss of the future we expected to have with our mate. We don't know what to expect or what is normal or acceptable emotions and behavior.

Divorce has become commonplace, even in the church. During the final editing of this book, I was reviewing some statistics by the Barna Research Group:

> After interviewing 3,142 randomly selected adults across the nation, including 1,220 born-again Christians, here are the key findings:
> Born again Christians are slightly more likely than non-Christians to go through a divorce. Twenty-seven percent of Christians have seen their marriage break up, compared to 23 percent of non-Christians.
> Adults who described themselves as Christian fundamentalists are more likely than others to get divorced: 30 percent have experienced divorce.
> Among adult Christians who have ever been divorced, 87 percent of those people experience their divorce after accepting Christ as their Savior.[1]

Invite participants to share feelings and reactions concerning their difficulty in dealing with divorce when appropriate and when there is time to fill.

Session 2

Briefly introduce returning journalers before a quick review of the last session. (New members should do session 1 at home rather than the entire group having to do the session over.)

Before reading journals aloud, encourage participants to begin to talk by sharing their past week. A simple, "How was your week?" or "Did you have any problems writing?" should get them primed to read aloud for the first time.

Ask for a volunteer to read from her journal. If no one offers, pick the person you believe will do it with ease. "Mary, would you be willing to begin?"

Take notes while the journals are being read. Have a brief discussion between each reading such as, "Anyone want to comment on what Mary just read?"

Turn to session 2: Discuss lifestyle changes that come after a divorce. See pages 28–30. Take turns reading aloud from those pages on "Identifying My Own Responses to Divorce."

Assign a review of their responses to divorce as a topic for journaling this week. Remember to inform the group that topic assignments are only suggestions. If participants feel the need to write about something else, they are free to do so. Suggest that journalers write more than one time during the week—especially when they are feeling emotional or depressed.

The rest of this session may be used in discussing which response to divorce they feel they are in, or you can move on to "Learning the Things I Really Didn't Want to Know," "Feelings," and "Fears." Encourage participants to reread the pages at home.

Ask for permission to make a list of names and telephone numbers to give out at the next session. It is important to never give out information without permission.

Session 3

Distribute the list of names and telephone numbers of consenting participants.

It is common for people to find encouragement in one another's writing, and they will probably ask for copies. Sharing losses and celebrating victories pave the way to survival. If no copying equipment is available on-site, ask the writer to make copies and bring them next time if he or she is comfortable doing that. Usually the recipients will gladly reimburse the 5 or 10 cents each copy costs.

Be sure to tell participants that it's okay to say no if they don't want to share copies of their work. Sometimes the things people write are such a delicate piece of their heart, they can't give it away.

Take turns reading the journaling done during the past week. Follow the same instructions for discussions as suggested in session 2. When that is finished, change the topic of discussion to "Facing Firsts," and begin session 3.

Many journalists have probably already talked or written about the words that seem difficult to say: *ex-wife*, *ex-husband*, *lonely*, *divorced*. They've probably discussed many "firsts." You'll need to decide if you want to ask them to read pages 44–47 aloud, or if an around-the-table discussion would be more appropriate at this time.

Suggest that everyone fill in the list of their support team to review when they feel all alone. Include family members, friends, neighbors, teachers, counselors, and even pets. Such a list can be revealing and show them that they are not as alone as they may feel. However, be aware of anyone who may need extra attention (new in town, no relatives, etc.).

There may be pain and possibly anger that will surface as you work through "Facing Reality" and "Facing Forgiveness." Be gentle. Not everyone will be ready to forgive. They should never be berated for that, only encouraged to seek God for help to let go of that which is negative and harmful.

"Shared Parenting" may be another discussion in which some participants may say, "No way!" This concept won't work for everyone. It is offered only as an option.

Have you been hugging and encouraging hugs at the end of each session? My friend, Marcia, says we need seven hugs a day to survive. Are you doing your part? Another friend jokingly commented to me, "The only time I get touched anymore is when I go to the chiropractor or the masseuse." While that might invoke a chuckle, there may be people in your group who feel exactly the same way.

Session 4

"How was your week?" is always a good way to open the session. It shouldn't take a lot of time, but it shows that you care about what is going on in the members' lives.

Remind journalers to make notes in their books about each other and what has worked in the divorce process—things they may want to remember.

Comment on the lined page at the end of each session called "Some things I'm thinking, feeling, wishing, hoping, doing." Encourage them to use these pages to write down any feelings they have, even those feelings of anger and disbelief.

Leaders, are you continuing to jot down things for discussion?

Sometimes, one person's journaling will seem to reveal a deeper intensity of grief than that expressed by others. This can have a minimizing effect on the grief of some in the group. Remind them that there is no stereotypical person dealing with divorce. There is no right or wrong feeling or behavior, or more painful divorce for one than another. All feelings are okay. Some people just express them more effectively and intensely.

Session 4 is the last chance participants will have to say something to or about the person they are divorcing during your time with them. Work through the chapter slowly. Read the letter on page 66 aloud and suggest that the question on the middle of page 67, "What would I want to say?" be answered when the person is alone and feels free to let their emotions flow onto paper.

A discussion about broken dreams offers a great opportunity to discuss an aspect of loss that Christians often try to avoid. Aren't we supposed to seek our dreams and decisions according to the will of God? What happens when it is a mate who disrupts God's will? Talk about it, and try to help the group members let go of some of the disappointments and broken promises.

It may be helpful to pass small pieces of paper for naming those disappointments and broken promises. Then pass a waste basket as a demonstration of letting go.

If time allows, discuss possible ways to hold on to some of their dreams, determining to still make them come true but without the person who was once a part of them.

The divorces in your journaling group may all be set in concrete. But if one family was restored as a result of the section on repairing the marriage, it is well worth its place in this book. Suggest that each person close their eyes for a moment and ask silently and for themselves only, "If I swallow my pride and offer to discuss reconciliation with my former mate, is there anything left to build on?" Remind them that God never wastes His children's pain. He can recycle or repair the broken pieces of that marriage, making it stronger than in the beginning. Sometimes, we need only to ask Him and then be obedient.

Most will probably assure you that there is "too much water under the bridge" and certainly, there may be. Don't push the reconciliation issue; just plant the seed, and let God do the rest.

Then, assign writing a letter as homework for the coming week. If participants have a problem with writing a letter to their former mate, suggest they write to one of those listed at the bottom of page 69.

Perhaps one of the most exciting things about being a leader is that you might have the privilege of leading someone to know Christ. You can deal with the section "A Step of Faith" in whatever way you are comfortable, but please don't ignore it. These people may never reconcile with a mate, but unless they reconcile with God, they will continue to live with a hole in their life.

This is also a good time to remind them that they are past the halfway mark through the sessions. Encourage friendships and telephone calls to others in the group and to friends and family outside the group. This will help them learn to depend on other support systems away from this group.

Session 5

Take time to hear stories of success and of failure from last week's difficult session. Then set the mood for the members to focus on themselves, on their future, and on ways to make life worthwhile and enjoyable again.

As you approach this chapter on creativity, be prepared to remind each person how they are a unique, creative, valuable gift from God. However, it sometimes takes breaking to release the creativity within. It is often out of pain that poetry or artistry flows.

Validation is a major need for someone dealing with a divorce. They need reassurance that life goes on even if they are no longer a husband or wife. Allow time to talk about that, if appropriate. Encourage working through their feelings with poetry and drawings at home.

Going around the room, have your group read aloud "Gifts to Consider" on page 87. Pause after each for a comment.

Page 89, "His Part, Our Part," offers an opportunity to discuss an aspect of divorce that Christians often avoid. Allow for time to talk about how bondage can block healing.

"Magic Moments" can and should be a turning point to positive thinking, positive attitudes, and positive moments when each allows healing to take over the once-raw edges of the divorce. From here on, focus on lovely things, celebrating, personal contentment, and delighting in God's plan for each person. Assure them that divorce has not ruined them for ministry, and God will use them if they will allow it.

Session 6

This may be one of your most special sessions. You and the others will be privileged to see drawings and hear poetry and music wrenched from pain deep within the soul. There may be laughter and tears as participants share the creativity that emerged from the past week's assignment.

Don't hurry through this. The divorced are giving each other "gifts of themselves" today, and healing is happening.

You will need to introduce "closure" with this session. No doubt, you have established a trusting relationship with the participants in this group, and that makes it difficult to say "good-bye" when the sessions are finished. Do this very gently. Divorce has already brought feelings of abandonment and rejection to participants, so care must be exercised to avoid the impression that you, too, are abandoning them.

Encourage them to continue writing in their journal after the sessions finish. Tell them that it is often the divorced who must do the reaching out to those friends who didn't know what to say. They can begin by making a telephone call, inviting someone to lunch, or organizing a hike or an evening at the movies.

Suggest that those without family support spend birthdays and holidays with a friend or someone in this group.

Ask if they are in touch with their church or synagogue. Is it time to rejoin a bowling team, a bridge club, or take a class at the local college? Is there a Bible study, a Saturday hiking group or fishing club? Can they sing in the church choir? Some may need a list of community activities to find a place to volunteer their talents.

In this session and the next, set the stage to thank them for the way they have touched and enriched your life. Tell them you are proud of them and the progress you've seen. By the end of this journey of journaling, most will have discovered that, though they can't turn the clock back, they can now wind it up again on their own.

Turn in your book to session 6. It is understandable that these people will dread those first holidays after the family unit is shattered. It will hurt when the children want to spend Christmas with both parents, not just one. Try to reassure them that most people find the "dreading it" was worse than the "doing it."

Pages 98–102 are good pages to read aloud. Talk about how they will spend the approaching holidays, anniversaries, and special days. Stress that it is okay to let go of old traditions and to let the day pass if needed.

Read the selection by Bill Butterworth aloud and allow time for comments.

Remind journalers that special days do not include only Thanksgiving and Christmas, birthdays and anniversaries. There will be Valentine's Day, Labor Day, the prom, graduation, and many special children's events that both parents might wish to attend. Discuss these as time allows.

Pass out any copies of articles on dealing with the holidays that you have on hand. Watch magazines for helpful articles to make copies of, but remember to write to the publisher or author for permission to do this. Most are copyrighted, making it unlawful to use the material without prior permission.

Session 7

Congratulate the returning participants for being willing to move on. It takes courage to squarely face an uncertain future.

Try to take no more than thirty minutes to hear what was written about holidays and special days.

It might be fun for this closing session to make up plastic bags as described on page 116 and give one to each participant sometime during this final session. Whether you do or not, turn to session 7, and ask the group to follow as you read about the Care Kit.

As you continue, keep the conversation and sharing open about the ways God uses imperfect people. There will be no homework since this is the final session, so ask the group to fill in the spaces as you work through the three ways to avoid despair and disappointment on pages 118–119.

Do the exercise on making lists of short-term and long-term goals on pages 121–122 during this session. Allow about ten minutes of quiet time for the group to write down some of their goals. Encourage them to discuss what they have written. Ask questions such as "How and when will you begin this goal?", "What help do you need, or can you do this alone?"

Talk about soloing and celebrating accomplished goals. Encourage them to tell someone about their victory. Ask each person to commit aloud to doing something fun for themselves within the next seven days.

This entire session should be done in class. Make it an upbeat meeting. Serve special refreshments (like peppermint ice cream), or tie balloons to the chairs before the group assembles.

Shake hands with each person as you give them a Certificate of Completion. (Use the certificate on page 131 to make as many photocopies as needed.)

Follow that with a hug!

Again, encourage participants to stay in touch with each other. Suggest they go back and reread what they wrote in the early sessions to see how far they have come. Close this session by praying for each person individually if you are comfortable doing that.

You will need to emotionally and physically detach from your group at this point if you plan to continue facilitating divorce recovery groups. Explain to the participants, if necessary, that you want them to find support and fellowship in each other, releasing you to reinvest your heart, time, and emotions in another group of hurting people.

Your help, love, and caring attitude will carry out into the community long after this journaling session is finished. If you want to stay in touch, or give permission for anyone to contact you, make that choice before saying "good-bye."

Your gift to these people has no doubt helped them to begin healing. For their continued healing, encourage them to study their Bible and get involved in church. God is the only one who can completely fill the void left by the person they are no longer married to.

(Note from author: A year after one of my groups finished the seven sessions, I invited them all to a buffet breakfast at my home. It was a time of rejoicing, hugging, and laughter as each person shared the events in their lives since finishing the journaling classes. What a treat for all of us to witness the transformation that had taken place in both the way they looked and their attitude about their place in life. I stood back for a while, just watching, listening, and marveling at the chatter and joy bouncing off my living room walls. It witnessed to a faithful God whose healing love covers every sorrow we commit to Him.)

Congratulations and thank you for helping others to rediscover the joy of living, even after the divorce from someone they'd hoped to share the rest of their life with. The time and love you have given is a priceless gift.

If you have questions or comments, you may write to the following address:.

> Barbara Baumgardner
> 2632 N.E. Rosemary Dr.
> Bend, OR 97701-9514
> E-mail address: barbarab@empnet.com

Leader's Notes:

Suggested Reading

Books

Anderson, Leith. *When God Says No*. Minneapolis: Bethany House, 1996.

Bustanoby, André. *But I Didn't Want a Divorce*. Grand Rapids, Mich.: Zondervan, 1978.

Butterworth, Bill. *When Life Doesn't Turn Out Like You Planned*. Nashville: Thomas Nelson, 1995.

Kniskern, Joseph Warren. *When the Vow Breaks*. Nashville: Broadman & Holman, 1993. Great

Osgood, Judy. *Meditations for the Divorced*. Sisters, Ore.: Gilgal Publications, 1987.

Smoke, Jim. *Growing through Divorce*. Eugene, Ore.: Harvest House, 1995.

Stanley, Charles. *Experiencing Forgiveness: An In Touch Study Series*. Nashville: Thomas Nelson, 1996.

Talley, Jim. *Reconcilable Differences: Mending Broken Relationships*. Nashville: Thomas Nelson, 1985.

Warnke, Michael and Rose Hall Warnke. *Recovering from Divorce*. Tulsa, Okla.: Victory House, 1992.

The Christian Daily Planner (annual): A journal to record events, devotional thoughts and prayers each day. Nashville: Word.

Periodicals

Christian Single Magazine, 127 9th Ave. N., Nashville, Tenn. 37234-0140 (615)251-5721. LifeWay Christian Resources. Encouragement for singles primarily in their 20s and 30s.

Single-Parent Family, 8605 Explorer Drive, Colorado Springs, Colo. 80920 (719)548-4588. Focus on the Family. To encourage and equip single parents to create stable, godly homes.

Endnotes

Session 1

1. Adapted from "A Death Has Occurred" by Reverend Paul Irion, quoted in Barbara Baumgardner, *A Passage through Grief: An Interactive Journal* (Nashville: Broadman & Holman, 1997), 2.

2. Wayne Oates, *Your Particular Grief* (Philadelphia: Westminster Press, 1981), 15.

3. Kahil Gibran, *The Wisdom of Gibran: Aphorisms and Maxims*, Joseph Sheban, ed. (New York: Philosophical Library, 1966), SP-ST-57.

4. Chris Cox, "What Is Divorce?" *Asheville* (N.C.) *Citizen Times*, 3 June 1997.

5. Michael A. Warnke and Rose Hall Warnke, *Recovering from Divorce* (Tulsa, Okla.: Victory House, 1992). John and Paula Sandford, *Restoring the Christian Family* (Tulsa, Okla.: Victory House Inc. 1980), 8, 21.

6. Jane Oja. Used by permission.

7. Joyce Lee, from her journals. Used by permission.

8. John Greenleaf Whittier, quoted in *Instant Quotation Dictionary* (Mundelein, Ill.: Career Institute), 223.

9. Charles H. Spurgeon, quoted in Sherwood Wirt and Kersten Beckstrom, eds., *Topical Encyclopedia of Living Quotations* (Minneapolis: Bethany House, 1982), 8:110.

10. Baumgardner, *A Passage through Grief*, 15.

11. Ibid., 15–16.

12. Quoted by Francis Thompson in *War Cry*, 21 May 1971, back cover.

13. Baumgardner, *A Passage through Grief*, 16.

14. Verdell Davis, quoted in *The Christian Daily Planner 1996* (Dallas: Word, 1996), 12 July 1996. All rights reserved.

Leader's Guide

1. George Barna, Barna Research Group, *The Barna Report* (Word Ministry Resources, September/October 1996), 5–6. From a study done in 1993. Used by permission of Barna Research.

Efforts have been made to locate and secure permission for all copyrighted material in this book. If you have any information on authors or credits omitted, we would appreciate receiving corrections so that proper acknowledgment can be give in future printings.

Write the author:

Barbara Baumgardner
2632 N.E. Rosemary Dr.
Bend, OR 97701-9514

E-mail: barbarab@empnet.com

or

Broadman & Holman Publishers
127 Ninth Avenue, North
Nashville, TN 37234

5. Bill Butterworth, *When Life Doesn't Turn Out Like You Planned* (Nashville: Thomas Nelson, 1995), 139–43. Used by permission of author.

6. John R. Rice, quoted in Wirt and Beckstrom, *Living Quotations*, 30:387.

7. Taken from the Dear Abby column, 16 December 1996, by Abigail Van Buren, copyright © Universal Press Syndicate. Reprinted with permission. All rights reserved.

8. Marianne K. Hering, "When Your Holidays Explode," *Virtue* (November/December 1996), 39. Used by permission of author.

9. Ibid., 39–40.

10. Bishop Remington, quoted in Wirt and Beckstrom, *Living Quotations*, 30:386.

Session 7

1. Donna Nevils, used by permission. Author of poem unknown.

2. Billy Graham, quoted in *The Daily Christian Planner 1996* (Dallas: Word, 1996), 17 March 1996. All rights reserved.

3. Graham, quoted in *The Daily Christian Planner 1996*, 29 April 1996. All rights reserved.

4. Denis Waitley, quoted in *The Daily Christian Planner 1997*, 13 February 1997. All rights reserved.

5. Lee, journals.

6. Joseph M. Stowell, "Frontlines," *Moody Magazine* (July/August 1997), 6. Used by permission.

Epilogue

1. Stowell, "Frontlines," 6.

2. Source unknown.

3. Harold S. Kushner, *When Bad Things Happen to Good People* (New York: Schocken Books, 1988), 127–28.

4. Jim Talley, *Reconcilable Differences* (Nashville: Thomas Nelson, 1985), 11. Web site: www.drtalley.com.

5. Ibid., 13.

6. Adapted from "Girl Most Likely to Succeed" in Judy Osgood, ed., *Meditations for the Divorced* (Sunriver, Ore.: Gilgal Publications, 1987), 62.

7. Barbara Johnson, quoted in *The Christian Daily Planner 1997* (Dallas: Word, 1997), 12 June 1997.

8. Davis, quoted in *The Christian Daily Planner 1997* (Dallas: Word, 1997), 1 July 1997.

Session 5

1. Martin Luther, quoted in Wirt and Beckstrom, *Living Quotations*, 161:2175.

2. Charles R. Swindoll, July 1996 ministry letter. Used by permission of Insight for Living.

3. Marilyn McGinnis, *Single* (Grand Rapids, Mich.: Fleming H. Revell, 1974), 94.

Session 6

1. Gail Brook Burket, "The Stepping-Stone Prayer," on bookmark by *Guideposts*, (Carmel, N. Y.). Used by permission of executor of Gail Brook Burket estate.

2. Lee, journals.

3. Adapted from Hospice of Bend, Ore., in Baumgardner, *A Passage through Grief*, 79–80.

4. Eugena Price, quoted in Wirt and Beckstrom, *Living Quotations*, 30:385.

Session 2

1. Elizabeth Kubler-Ross, *On Death and Dying* (New York: Macmillan, 1969).

2. Davis, quoted in *The Christian Daily Planner 1997* (Dallas: Word, 1997), March 1997, preface.

3. Author unknown, quoted in Wirt and Beckstrom, *Living Quotations*, 26:339.

4. Charles R. Swindoll, *Growing Strong in the Seasons of Life* (Grand Rapids, Mich.: Zondervan, 1983), 166–67.

5. Lee, journals.

6. Henry Gariepy, quoted in *The Christian Daily Planner 1996* (Dallas: Word, 1996), 1 January 1996.

7. Lee, journals.

Session 3

1. Ruth Graham Bell, *Sitting by My Laughing Fire* (Dallas: Word, 1977), 11. All rights reserved.

2. Author unknown.

3. Lee, journals.

4. Charles Stanley, *Experiencing Forgiveness* (Nashville: Thomas Nelson, 1996), ix.

5. Susan Reimer, "Forgiveness," *Baltimore Sun*, Baltimore, Md., 7 June 1996. Used by permission of the *Baltimore Sun*.

6. Ibid.

Session 4

1. Chinese proverb, source unknown.

2. Excerpts from letter written to husband by author.

Endnotes

Session 1

1. Adapted from "A Death Has Occurred" by Reverend Paul Irion, quoted in Barbara Baumgardner, *A Passage through Grief: An Interactive Journal* (Nashville: Broadman & Holman, 1997), 2.

2. Wayne Oates, *Your Particular Grief* (Philadelphia: Westminster Press, 1981), 15.

3. Kahil Gibran, *The Wisdom of Gibran: Aphorisms and Maxims,* Joseph Sheban, ed. (New York: Philosophical Library, 1966), SP-ST-57.

4. Chris Cox, "What Is Divorce?" *Asheville* (N.C.) *Citizen Times,* 3 June 1997.

5. Michael A. Warnke and Rose Hall Warnke, *Recovering from Divorce* (Tulsa, Okla.: Victory House, 1992). John and Paula Sandford, *Restoring the Christian Family* (Tulsa, Okla.: Victory House Inc. 1980), 8, 21.

6. Jane Oja. Used by permission.

7. Joyce Lee, from her journals. Used by permission.

8. John Greenleaf Whittier, quoted in *Instant Quotation Dictionary* (Mundelein, Ill.: Career Institute), 223.

9. Charles H. Spurgeon, quoted in Sherwood Wirt and Kersten Beckstrom, eds., *Topical Encyclopedia of Living Quotations* (Minneapolis: Bethany House, 1982), 8:110.

10. Baumgardner, *A Passage through Grief,* 15.

11. Ibid., 15–16.

12. Quoted by Francis Thompson in *War Cry,* 21 May 1971, back cover.

13. Baumgardner, *A Passage through Grief,* 16.

14. Verdell Davis, quoted in *The Christian Daily Planner 1996* (Dallas: Word, 1996), 12 July 1996. All rights reserved.

Suggested Reading

Books

Anderson, Leith. *When God Says No*. Minneapolis: Bethany House, 1996.

Bustanoby, André. *But I Didn't Want a Divorce*. Grand Rapids, Mich.: Zondervan, 1978.

Butterworth, Bill. *When Life Doesn't Turn Out Like You Planned*. Nashville: Thomas Nelson, 1995.

Kniskern, Joseph Warren. *When the Vow Breaks*. Nashville: Broadman & Holman, 1993. Great

Osgood, Judy. *Meditations for the Divorced*. Sisters, Ore.: Gilgal Publications, 1987.

Smoke, Jim. *Growing through Divorce*. Eugene, Ore.: Harvest House, 1995.

Stanley, Charles. *Experiencing Forgiveness: An In Touch Study Series*. Nashville: Thomas Nelson, 1996.

Talley, Jim. *Reconcilable Differences: Mending Broken Relationships*. Nashville: Thomas Nelson, 1985.

Warnke, Michael and Rose Hall Warnke. *Recovering from Divorce*. Tulsa, Okla.: Victory House, 1992.

The Christian Daily Planner (annual): A journal to record events, devotional thoughts and prayers each day. Nashville: Word.

Periodicals

Christian Single Magazine, 127 9th Ave. N., Nashville, Tenn. 37234-0140 (615)251-5721. LifeWay Christian Resources. Encouragement for singles primarily in their 20s and 30s.

Single-Parent Family, 8605 Explorer Drive, Colorado Springs, Colo. 80920 (719)548-4588. Focus on the Family. To encourage and equip single parents to create stable, godly homes.